M000026183

THE COMPLETE GUIDE TO WHOODLES

Jordan Honeycutt

LP Media Inc. Publishing

For information address LP Media Inc. Publishing, 3178 253rd Ave. NW, Isanti, MN 55040

www.lpmedia.org

Publication Data

Jordan Honeycutt

The Complete Guide to Whoodles – First edition.

Summary: "Successfully raising a Whoodle Dog from puppy to old age" – Provided by publisher.

ISBN: 978-1-954288-09-6

[1. Whoodle – Non-Fiction] I. Title.

Design by Sorin Rădulescu
First hardcover edition, 2021
Cover Photo Courtesy of Bethany McCue

TABLE OF CONTENTS

CHAPTER 9

Training Your Whoodle

CHAPTER 10

Traveling with Your Whoodle

CHAPTER 11

Grooming Your Whoodle

CHAPTER 14

CHAPTER 15

Special Thanks

A special thank you goes out to Meryl Siegman for all her hard work in helping us create this book. Her experience, knowledge and personal stories of her life with Willow have helped to add an intimate look into the day-to-day life of a Whoodle owner.

An additional thank you also needs to be given to Deborah Gaynor for sharing her own personal stories from her Whoodle Flynn for the book.

Stories about both Willow and Flynn will appear periodically throughout the following pages and we hope that their experiences will help illustrate the concepts and ideas that are written about, giving you a deeper understanding of life living with a Whoodle.

CHAPTER 1
Breed History

What Is a Whoodle?

The Whoodle, while not an official dog breed yet, is still making an impact. A cross between a Soft-Coated Wheaten Terrier and a Poodle, this lovable dog is playful, friendly, active and highly intelligent. Also referred to as Wheatenpoos, Wheatendoodles, or Sweatenpoos, Whoodles make the perfect companion for adults and kids alike.

Often called toddlers in teddy bear suits, these dogs are full of joy and love that they light up a room with boundless, playful energy. Unlike some of the more temperamental Terriers, Whoodles are non-aggressive and excellent with children. Bred in small, medium and large sizes, these show-stopping living teddy bears are basically the quintessential family pet.

Photo Courtesy of Amy Rizer

History of the Whoodle

The origins of the Whoodle are largely unknown, but it is thought that the two parent breeds were first crossed in the 1990s. Rising to popularity in the early 2000s, the Whoodle is now becoming a staple in the crossbreed designer-dog world. In high demand today, breeders often have long wait lists just to purchase a puppy.

> **FUN FACT**
> **What is a Designer Dog?**
>
> Whoodles are considered a designer or hybrid breed, but what does that mean? A designer dog breed is a result of combining two purebred dogs, in this case, a soft-coated Wheaten Terrier and a Poodle. Purebreds are dogs from a breed that is recognized by an official kennel club and who have been the same breed over many generations. As of 2020, the American Kennel Club (AKC) will not recognize any new breeds that are the result of two AKC-registered breeds, but these dogs are eligible to be registered as AKC Canine Partners.

After the introduction of other Poodle hybrid dogs, such as the Labradoodle and the Cockapoo, in the United States, people began breeding to produce different-sized dogs with similar hypoallergenic qualities and intelligence. This movement has given rise to many "doodles," including the Whoodle.

To better understand the Whoodle, let's take a look at the crossbreed's parents of origin. Depending on breeding, this dog can take on the character traits of either breed. You can read more about generations and subsequent traits further on in this chapter.

SOFT-COATED WHEATEN TERRIER – The Soft-Coated Wheaten Terrier is one of four Terrier breeds native to Ireland. According to the American Kennel Club, legend claims "when the Spanish Armada sunk off the coast of Ireland, the blue dogs on the ships swam ashore and were welcomed by wheaten-colored Terriers. Breeding between these dogs is supposed to have produced the Kerry Blue Irish Terrier."

Needless to say, this is a very old dog breed. Since only the gentry were allowed to own hounds, spaniels and Beagles, commoners enlisted the services of the Soft-Coated Wheaten Terrier instead. As a result, the Wheaten Terrier became known as the "poor man's wolfhound." Bred to be a hard-working farm dog, the Wheaten Terrier's job included herding, guarding livestock, and hunting and killing vermin.

Today, Soft-Coated Wheaten Terriers can be found performing various tasks such as herding, agility and even diving. In fact, a Soft-Coated Wheaten Terrier

Soft-Coated Wheaten Terrier

named Krista earned one first-place and two third-place ribbons in preliminary diving competitions before the national dog diving championship finals in 2016.

Standing 17 to 20 inches tall and weighing 30 to 45 pounds, the Soft-Coated Wheaten Terrier is a medium sized dog with a square structure. Their hair is soft and silky and does not shed. It does need regular trimming and frequent brushing to keep it healthy and free of mats.

Soft-Coated Wheaten Terrier puppies are born with dark coats that turn various shades of wheat color as they mature. Rarely, you may find a red or black Wheaten Terrier, but not often.

Full of life, these dogs have high energy, a very playful nature and above-average intelligence. They are also typically less aggressive than other Terrier breeds and can get along well with other pets and species, especially if introduced early. With all of these great qualities, it's no wonder they are a popular breed to cross with the Poodle.

POODLE – Although it is the national dog of France, the Poodle actually originated in Germany. Bred to be water-loving retrievers, these dogs were used to bring birds and ducks back to their owners while hunting. Although our cultural view of the Poodle has changed over the years, the breed has not lost its athletic ability or its retriever skill and is still used frequently out in the field.

Due to the Poodle's excellent trainability and flashy looks, this breed was prized in noble households in Europe and eventually became a well-known part of the European circus. One of the most intelligent dog breeds, the Poodle has proved itself highly useful throughout its history.

While the image of a well-groomed Poodle may bring up notions of an aloof, high-strung, a little bit too-good-for-you dog as portrayed in movies and pop culture, the fashionable Poodle cut is actually one that originated out of function. Less hair meant more efficiency in the water but left the dog susceptible to the cold. Leaving hair around the torso and joints protected the dog's vulnerable areas from the cold water while still making swimming easier.

The Toy and Miniature Poodles were bred down in size from the Standard Poodle in the early 20th century in America in order to adapt the beloved breed to better suit city dwellers. Although the Toy Poodle is now more of a lap and companion dog, the breed still retains the superior intelligence and athletic abilities of its ancestors. Regardless of size, all Poodles must follow the same breed standards.

Standard Poodle

With non-shedding coats, Poodles are another breed that needs regular coat trims and brushing. Like Soft-Coated Wheaten Terriers, Poodles can make wonderful companions to all, but training is very important for this intelligent, proud and sometimes stubborn breed.

Physical Characteristics

Due to the breed's very short history, many Whoodles are produced by breeding a Poodle to a Soft-Coated Wheaten Terrier, resulting in a first-generation Whoodle. For these reasons, Whoodles can vary in appearance greatly from breeder to breeder. Because the Whoodle is a crossbreed, it is not recognized by the American Kennel Club and therefore no breed standard exists. Even so, there are a few key features that are typically present in a Whoodle.

Depending on what type of Poodle a dog was bred from, Whoodles range from small to large in size. They typically stand anywhere from 12 and 20 inches tall, weighing 20 to 45 pounds, but can also become much larger depending on the parent dogs. If your Whoodle was bred with a Toy or Miniature Poodle, expect him to be much smaller at maturity than one bred from a Standard Poodle.

Tail docking is somewhat controversial among Whoodle breeders and owners. Some breeders automatically dock the tails of their Whoodle puppies, and some give you a choice as to remove your dog's tail or not. Docking was originally performed for reasons of functionality and safety.

Believe it or not, people used to believe docking a dog's tail would prevent the dog from getting rabies. A farm dog's tail was also docked to prevent it from becoming injured or infected after picking up burrs and other hazards on the ground. Some believed that a tail could prevent a guard dog from defending his territory because it would give the attacker something to grab.

Regardless of the reason tails were docked historically, today the purpose is mostly cosmetic. There is no health benefit to remove a dog's tail and the reality is, it causes the dog a great deal of pain. Talk to your breeder about the benefits and drawbacks to tail docking before you make a decision on behalf of your new Whoodle.

The coat of the Whoodle is medium length and comes in many varieties. Just like its parent breeds, the Whoodle has hair and not fur. It can be any texture from straight and silky to curly. Since the Poodle can produce a wide variety of coat colors, the Whoodle can also appear in almost any color combination, with any markings. Black, brown, red, silver, grey and cream are the most common colors seen. Some Whoodles can even be spotted.

Photo Courtesy of
Cristi Tombrello
Photo by Heather Kemp

Generations of Whoodles

You may think that all Whoodles are the same, but that is far from the truth. As mentioned earlier, due to the relative novelty of the crossbreed, many Whoodles are a product of first-generation crossing, pairing a Wheaten Terrier with a Poodle. However, some breeders choose to breed Whoodle to Poodle, Whoodle to Wheaten and even Whoodle to Whoodle. These cross-bred dogs are labeled F1, F2, F3, F1b and F2b.

Each generation can produce its own traits and characteristics depending on genetics. Here is a breakdown and basic definition of each.

F1 - These dogs are first-generation Whoodles, produced by breeding a Soft-Coated Wheaten Terrier and a Poodle. Genetically, this produces offspring that are 50% Poodle and 50% Wheaten Terrier.

F2 - Produced by breeding two F1 Whoodles, F2 dogs are simply the cross of two first generation Whoodles.

Photo Courtesy of Dria Lobosco

F3 – F3s are produced by breeding two F2 Whoodles. Anything after F3 is called "multi-generational" breeding. When compared to an F1b (see below), F3 and multi-generational Doodles have less predictable characteristics, since they will have a greater diversity of genetics from both parent breeds.

F1B – These dogs are produced by breeding an F1 (first generation Whoodle) to a purebred dog, either a Wheaten or a Poodle. The resulting genetics are approximately 25%/75% with the genetics of the purebred dog taking over the majority.

For example, if an F1 Whoodle is bred to a Poodle, the offspring would be 75% Poodle, 25% Wheaten Terrier. If an F1 Whoodle is bred to a Wheaten Terrier, the offspring would be 75% Wheaten Terrier and 25% Poodle.

F2B – This is the result of crossing an F2 back to a purebred Poodle or Wheaten Terrier, or by crossing an F1b to a F1.

When searching for a Whoodle puppy, talk to your breeder about which traits and qualities they breed for in each generation. This can involve personality as well as physical characteristics.

Typical Breed Behavior

Just as with the Whoodle's appearance, there is no breed standard for behavior. However, given what we know about the Poodle and the Soft-Coated Wheaten Terrier, we can predict general breed behavior possibilities.

Whoodles are highly intelligent, loving and affectionate to their owners. Because most designer dogs are bred solely for companion purposes, Whoodles are heavily dependent on their owners for interaction and want to be around them whenever possible. Interestingly, though they love their people, Whoodles are still not likely to suffer from separation anxiety.

Photo Courtesy of Kristen Londoño

Active dogs, Whoodles will never pass on a good time, a hike outdoors, or a game of fetch. That said, Whoodles do not need excessive amounts of intense exercise and will adapt well to a less adventurous lifestyle as long as they get plenty of active play time.

The Terrier side of this crossbred dog gives the Whoodle its high energy and bold nature. The Poodle parent contributes to the breed's high intelligence and excellent trainability, and also to its sometimes stubborn nature. Whoodles are highly responsive to praise when training but often think they know best and will not respond to harsh or forceful training. Patience is a virtue Whoodle owners will need in abundance, especially while training.

Relatively quiet dogs, Whoodles often will not even bark at strangers. While this can be a major bonus for city dwellers who need a quiet dog, it does not make for a particularly good watch dog.

Whoodles also possess a strong prey drive due to their history as working farm dogs and inherited Terrier instinct. They will often chase small animals such as mice, rabbits and squirrels. This instinctual behavior may require extensive training to control.

Stories from a Whoodle Owner

Whoodle Characteristics

Willow

When I picked Willow up from the breeder in April, 2019, neither of us fully realized at the time our lives would be changed forever. It's been a wonderful journey.

Willow is the quintessential Whoodle: smart, beautiful, devoted, happy, loving and friendly. She loves everyone: babies, kids, grown-ups, puppies and dogs, and she loves everything: getting in the car, going to the vet, visiting my mom. Everything is an adventure.

She is mischievous and has a great sense of humor. She loves grabbing a shoe or a sock and running around with it, wanting to be chased. But I think what I adore most about her is her ability to communicate. She has numerous barks, whoofs, grunts, rumbles and high-pitched songs, mostly utterances of unfettered joy. Her facial expressions and body movements are endlessly expressive. She wags her tail in her sleep. Her ability to understand is equally profound. I don't think there is anything she doesn't comprehend.

Is a Whoodle the Right Choice for You?

If you're looking for a beautiful, non-shedding, energetic companion that looks like a real-life teddy bear, the Whoodle may be the perfect dog for you. Loyal and always down for a good time, a Whoodle could be the companion you've been hoping for.

Whoodles offer friendship to everyone they encounter and do well with children of all ages. Children can benefit greatly from caring for a dog, but they must be trained to properly handle a Whoodle so they do not harm a small pup.

The scrappy, yet friendly nature of these dogs helps them play the role of family pet with energetic passion, but it is still wise to be careful with small children as they can sometimes injure smaller dogs and puppies unintentionally with extra tight hugs or too-firm pats. Always teach your children to be gentle so they don't accidentally injure your Whoodle. Luckily, the Whoodle is not delicately built and can handle a bit more roughness than other breeds.

Whoodles need both a lot of physical activity and a lot of time with their owners. That, paired with high grooming demands, makes this a dog for only the most dedicated of owners. Companionship and loyal care are of the utmost importance for the Whoodle and your dog will suffer if he does not receive it.

As long as you can provide your dog with the physical activity he requires, he should be able to adapt well to city life. It may, however, be easier to meet these requirements if you choose a mini Whoodle versus a standard size.

It is worth noting that climate may also affect the well-being of your Whoodle. While they love snow and thrive in cold weather, they can suffer greatly from the heat. Their heat intolerance makes them more suitable for homes in colder climates.

Although Whoodles are generally healthier than their pure-bred counterparts, there are some health issues that affect both the Soft-Coated Wheaten Terrier and the Poodle. This is something you should be prepared to handle before adopting a dog from this breed. These health conditions will be discussed in greater detail in Chapter 13.

Before bringing your Whoodle home, it's important to carefully consider all aspects of ownership. Taking on a dog of any breed presents challenges and frustrations. Can you afford to care for your dog? Do you have the time to devote to it? Are there any restrictions where you live? If you are willing to properly prepare for the dog you choose, the transition into dog parenthood should be a smooth one.

CHAPTER 2

Choosing Your Whoodle

Buying Versus Adopting

Deciding whether to purchase your Whoodle from a breeder or adopt from a rescue is a tough decision. We all have our hearts pricked when we see dogs in need but oftentimes these dogs have special needs, medical or social, and require a special kind of home. If you think you can provide the patience and care it may take to adopt a rescue Whoodle, please do so! The dog will reward you with love and companionship just as much as one you purchase from a breeder.

One benefit to adopting or purchasing an older Whoodle is knowing the dog's personality before you bring him home. Does the dog enjoy the company of young children or other dogs? What level of exercise does this particular dog expect? Also, many social or medical issues may be apparent, so you know exactly what challenges the dog's health will present. There are very few surprises when it comes to adopting a well-established, older Whoodle.

Not only are you eliminating many of the unknowns of purchasing a young puppy, but rescue dogs seem to show a special appreciation for a new chance at a forever home. If you're looking to adopt a Whoodle and happen to find one at a rescue, chances are the dog will be adopted fast, so don't waste time getting your application in to take him home.

HELPFUL TIP
Which Size?

Whoodles can come in a variety of sizes, depending mostly on how big or small the Poodle parent was. While Wheaten Terriers usually weigh between 30 to 40 pounds, Poodles can vary in size from Toy to Miniature to Standard, spanning a weight range of four pounds up to 70 pounds. To determine approximately how large your Whoodle will grow, take the average of the two parents.

On the other hand, purchasing a young puppy from a breeder carries with it a unique set of challenges and joys. One apparent difference is cost factor. Adopting is typically much less expensive upfront than purchasing from a breeder. While adopting fees range from location to location, it is typically no more than a few hundred dollars while a breeder can charge up to $2,500.

Another aspect to consider is raising your dog through the puppy phase. Those tiny, fluffy faces may seem sweet, but a rowdy puppy can wreak havoc and present frustrating challenges until he reaches maturity around the age of two. Of course, puppies bring joy as well and with proper socialization and training, even the rowdiest puppies can develop into wonderful companions. While it is hard and sometimes frustrating work, raising a puppy from 8 weeks old allows you to ensure that he becomes properly socialized and trained during those crucial early weeks.

Photo Courtesy of Bethany McCue

Photo Courtesy of Kalin Smith

Importance of Breeder Reputation

If you choose the breeder route, finding a trustworthy breeder can be a challenge. The price tag on a "designer" dog such as a Whoodle can be high, and this has caused many to take up what is commonly called backyard breeding. These breeders often do little or no testing to ensure the health of their litters. Some of these places may even be puppy mills, where dogs are kept in cages to do nothing more than produce litter after litter. This is a terrible life for a dog! Not supporting places like this is just as important as ensuring the health of your puppy.

A good, reputable breeder will be known in the Whoodle breeder community. They will undoubtedly have connections with other reputable breeders. If you find a good breeder who has no available puppies, you may want to contact them and ask for the names of other breeders in the area. A reputable breeder is always concerned with breeding healthy dogs and should only recommend breeders who do the same. Finding a breeder who specializes in Whoodles will also help ensure that your breeder is devoted to developing and improving the breed by producing healthy pups.

Stories from a Whoodle Owner

Willow

An "In-Demand" Breed

Whoodles are in such demand, most of the country's top breeders have waiting lists for litters that are not even born yet. Your best bet is to commit to a breeder and get on a list right away by providing the necessary information and putting down a deposit, which is usually non-refundable. You get to choose your newborn Whoodle based on when you placed your deposit, which determines what number you are on the waiting list.

After deciding a Whoodle was the right breed for me, I quickly realized I had to abandon the fantasy of meeting a litter of happy, bouncy 8-week-old Whoodle pups and getting to pick the one that appealed to me the most. I discovered I had to choose my life-long companion based on a tiny image of little one-pound blobs sent to me over the internet. I was Number 3 on the list for Willow's upcoming litter of mini-Whoodles.

There were 9 puppies in the litter. Because my preference was for a female, I got to choose among one black and two blonde puppies. There are three factors in choosing your new Whoodle pup this way: gender, color and markings. So, start thinking about the color and sex of your ideal puppy. I chose the black one. I can't say little Willow winked at me, because her eyes were still not open, but nevertheless something about her really spoke to me.

Photo Courtesy of Carmen Gonzalez NYCPET Pawtographer

Finding the Right Breeder

The internet makes finding a reputable breeder easier than ever and yet challenging at the same time. It can easily become information overload. If you do a quick internet search for "Whoodle puppies for sale," you will find many breeders. Some of these, no doubt, you will want to avoid. How can you tell the difference between a reputable breeder and someone who is just in it for the money without any care for the well-being of the dogs?

One great way to source a good breeder is to ask around. If you know someone with a Whoodle, don't be afraid to ask where they got the dog and how their experience was. Spot an adorable Whoodle across the park? Approach the owner and inquire about the dog and their breeder. Enthusiastic Whoodle owners should be thrilled to share their breeder's information with others.

Yelp can also be a great tool to weed out shady breeders. While reviews can be biased, a breeder with negative reviews is probably best eliminated from the list or at the very least worth deeper investigation before purchasing.

When choosing a breeder, ask how their puppies are raised. Are they kept in a kennel or are they raised in a home with lots of early social interaction? The more they are handled in the first several weeks, the better. Your breeder should also be willing to send you regular photo and even email updates on your pup as he grows from birth until he comes home.

Health Tests and Certifications

There are several questions you should ask any breeder when you are searching for the perfect Whoodle puppy.

CAN I VISIT THE BREEDING FACILITY? The answer to this question should always be a resounding yes. A breeder might not allow you into certain areas of the facility for the safety of the puppies. They could be concerned about tracking in diseases that could be detrimental to a young puppy's undeveloped immune system. However, a quality breeder should always allow you to come on-site and see other dogs in their program. If they refuse, this could be a sign they have something to hide and you should reconsider dealing with them.

HOW LONG HAVE YOU BEEN BREEDING WHOODLES? You should only buy from an experienced breeder who is well established. A quality breeder who has several years of experience will know all the ins and outs of breeding for only the most desirable traits and healthy dogs.

WHAT GENETIC CONDITIONS DO YOU TEST FOR BEFORE BREEDING AND WHAT CONDITIONS DO YOU SCREEN THE PUPPIES FOR BEFORE SELLING? There are numerous genetic conditions that Poodles and Soft-Coated Wheaten Terriers are prone to developing, which are discussed in detail in Chapter 13. Before agreeing to purchase a puppy, ask for a detailed list of the tests the breeder had performed on the parents, and ask for copies of the test results. These tests should be performed by certified specialists for each potential ailment, such as a board-certified veterinarian cardiologist and an ophthalmologist.

CAN I SEE VETERINARY RECORDS FOR BOTH PARENTS? When investing your time and money into a Whoodle puppy, you will want to have an open and transparent line of communication with your chosen breeder. If the breeder is not willing to share medical records of the puppy's parents, this may be a signal that you should find another breeder. Both the dam and

Photo Courtesy of Liz O'Brien

Photo Courtesy of Jazmin Ruiz-Sorkin

the sire should have been checked by specialists and cleared of having any defects. The breeder should also provide proof of genetic testing.

WHAT KIND OF GUARANTEE DO YOU PROVIDE FOR YOUR PUPPIES? A good breeder will always guarantee the health of their puppies. Look for guarantees that will refund most or all of the cost of the puppy in the event any congenital health conditions appear within the first year. Beware of breeders who only offer to replace the puppy with a healthy one with no option to receive a refund instead.

If the breeder sold you a genetically unhealthy puppy the first time, you won't want to bring home a second puppy from the facility. Many are also unwilling to return their dog for a replacement, as they have already become attached. This is a low-risk guarantee from a breeder and may be a warning sign. A responsible breeder will always take back a dog that you can no longer care for, no matter the reason. In fact, many require this in the purchase agreement.

Many times, a breeder's health guarantee will have stipulations. These may include not neutering or spaying until after a year so that the dog's joints are allowed to fully develop, feeding your puppy a proper diet, and regular visits to the vet. As much as a responsible breeder wants their puppies to remain in perfect health for their entire life, not all owners care for a dog the same way, and health results will vary based on lifestyle.

Remember, no matter how good the breeding lines are or how thorough the testing, no breeder can guarantee perfect health for a dog's entire life. If something does go wrong with your puppy, it is important to understand any lifestyle factors before blaming the breeder.

DO YOU EVER SELL TO A BROKER OR PET SHOP? If the answer is yes, do not support this breeder. A responsible breeder breeds for the betterment of the dog's health and appearance and will never sell one of their dogs to a broker or a pet store. Reputable breeders care for their pups and typically want to meet the families of each of their dogs to be sure they will be properly cared for. Dogs found in a pet shop are bred solely for profit and never come with a health guarantee.

Stories from a Whoodle Owner

Flynn the Whoodle

I knew we needed a hypoallergenic dog, to keep the wheezing and sneezing from taking over our lives. There are a number of hypo-allergenic and non-shedding dogs if you are serious about your search, but I had always wanted a standard poodle, and knew that a poodle hybrid was going to be the right fit for our lifestyle. Soon we were pointed in the direction of a Poodle-Terrier hybrid, and size and personality were the next considerations. The enormous Schnoodles (a cross between a Standard Poodle and a Standard Schnauzer) were tempting, but the reality of being in our mid-60s was that an aging large dog was not going to get the physical support needed from an aging couple. The perfectly sized (40-45 pounds) Standard Whoodle brought the added benefit of the glorious Wheaten person-ality (FUN! Whoodles just want to have fun!), and our search narrowed to finding a reputable breeder within driving distance, and with an available puppy in the right time frame. When we arrived to receive that precious package of wriggles, it was love at first sight.

At 8 weeks old, Flynn sported the stunning silky brown and black coat of a chocolate brin-dle, with a white chest blaze and front paws that looked like he had tip-toed through fresh white paint. We were entranced as we held him for the first time. Flynn proudly showed off his leash skills during our many stops on the 10 hour drive home, taking potty breaks just like a big dog!

Photo Attribution - Crista Oberkirch - www.cristaoberkirch.com Head to Tail Dog Grooming

Break over, he drank a little water, nibbled some food, played with his new chew toy, and mostly napped happily for most of that long car ride.

The value of choosing a good breeder was immediately apparent, when Flynn easily settled into his crate for his first night at home, and slept right through the night. We had lucked into a puppy with a strong bladder! The next day was much more of a challenge; we had to learn Flynn's signals, and he had to develop ways to communicate with us. We all were exhausted that second night, but Flynn's joyous approach to everything never faltered.

When our mobile vet came for his "well puppy" check two days later, she sat on the living room floor after emptying her shoulder bag of stethoscope and other tools. Flynn promptly grabbed the strap and proudly dragged the bag over to her--and to this day, he still loves dragging anything with a strap. She took one look at him, and exclaimed, "what a little extrovert!". She nailed it--Flynn loves people, children, other dogs, cats, birds, toys, and treats. He is convinced that anyone who comes to the door is there to see him, and to love him, and he's usually right, even if they thought they were stopping by for another reason.

Flynn demonstrates the classic Wheaten Terrier aerial spin expressing overwhelming joy whenever he sees a favorite friend--person or dog. His happiness is infectious; you have to laugh with him, and share his pleasure. He uses that spin to invite other dogs to play if they're being a little shy or sluggish. When he sees an old friend on the other side of a door or fence, he greets them from several feet up in the air, spinning excitedly, with his tail wagging so hard it propels him around.

Breeder Contracts and Guarantees

Many breeders require buyers to sign a contract that outlines what is and isn't acceptable to do with the dog. The average contract defines the payment amount for the Whoodle puppy and determines what happens if you can no longer keep the dog. Most breeders require that you return the Whoodle instead of giving the dog to a rescue or animal shelter.

Some breeder contracts also require that you spay or neuter your dog, often within a certain time frame. As more research comes out, breeders are more often stipulating that you wait until after the dog is fully mature, between 12 and 18 months old, before sterilizing to help prevent certain diseases, including bone cancer.

Ask the breeder if any genetic testing is included in the contract and if so, which ones? See Chapter 13 for a more detailed list of genetic conditions you should ask the breeder if the dam and sire have been tested for.

Raising Multiple Puppies from the Same Litter

Sometimes people get the notion that they should bring home not one, but two puppies from a litter. They may believe that the dogs can keep each other company while they're at work. They may want to get a puppy for each child. They may even decide to get two puppies because they just can't pick between the dogs! While these may seem like valid reasons at first glance, you may want to reconsider.

Most breeders warn against getting two puppies at the same time, especially from the same litter. The work of caring for one puppy is hard, but the work of caring for two puppies can become quickly overwhelming. Each puppy will need to be crated, played with, and trained separately. There will be twice the mess and accidents to clean up, too.

It is true that the puppies will most likely grow up to be best friends. However, this often happens at the expense of the dog-owner relationship. The two dogs will create an inseparable bond that you cannot compete with.

A reputable breeder should always advise against getting two puppies at the same time. In fact, most will actually refuse to sell multiples. If you really want two dogs, it is best to get them at different times. Establish a bond with one dog then if you want another, repeat the bonding process with the second before the two are allowed to pair up. This bond can be achieved by spending quality time alone with your dog as often as possible. Even so, many people find that two dogs together will develop a bond that could potentially take away from the one shared between you and them.

Picking the Perfect Puppy

Although temperament and behavioral characteristics should be relatively consistent throughout a litter of Whoodles, this crossbreed can produce puppies with a variety of personalities. Depending on generation and lineage, as discussed in chapter one, one puppy may take on more of a Poodle personality and another more of a Soft-Coated Wheaten Terrier.

If possible, you may want to visit your breeder's facility to pick out your new puppy. Often, however, breeders have waiting lists of people hoping to purchase a puppy from their next litter and choices are made based on photographs of very young pups, sometimes even at a single day old. In this common scenario, you are essentially choosing your Whoodle pup based on color and sex.

Whether you are able to choose your pick of the litter in person or via photograph, once you have chosen a reputable breeder, it is important to get on the list as soon as possible. This will allow you the best possible chance of getting an early pick from the litter making it more likely you will get the sex and color you desire.

If you are lucky enough to be able to visit the litter beforehand, consider the following puppy personality types when selecting your perfect puppy. If you are unsure which puppy you should choose, ask the breeder for help. They have spent the most time with the puppies and should have a good idea of each of their personalities.

Male Versus Female

There is very little apparent behavioral difference between a spayed female and a neutered male. In fact, trainers claim that the behavior of these dogs is more dependent on how they are raised and trained.

Although lifelong behavior may be similar between a neutered male and a spayed female, the female dog will reach maturity quicker than the male, making her potentially easier to train at an earlier age. Also, it is worth noting that a female dog, on average, is slightly smaller than a male. If you are concerned about size, this may sway you toward one sex or another.

If you do not plan to spay or neuter your Whoodle, there are a few more considerations to factor in before you make a decision. An intact male will likely mark his territory, outside or even in your home. He may also hump more frequently and may be more likely to wander off in search of a mate. These are natural, yet unwanted characteristics to think about when it comes to choosing the perfect family pet.

An unspayed female Whoodle will go into "heat" about twice a year. This is when she will be able to conceive and carry puppies. During this time, she will secrete a vaginal discharge that can be bloody and lasts 2 to 6 weeks. If you plan to choose a female pup and not spay her, be prepared to give her special care and attention during this time.

While there are anecdotal tales of differences, studies and trainers suggest that outside of the biological and physical differences, both sexes behave similarly and can make excellent family pets. Decide which scenario best suits what you are looking for and choose that one.

The Different Puppy Personality Types

Most puppies fit into one of 5 categories.

THE DOMINANT PUPPY – This puppy could be bossy, pushy, and possibly more vocal than the others. He may be more rebellious and challenging to train. These puppies can potentially have behavior problems later in life if they aren't trained early.

THE ACTIVE PUPPY – Active puppies can be somewhat pushy and bossy and sometimes a little mouthy. They are typically high-energy dogs that get excited very easily. They can get easily distracted, which can make training more of a challenge.

THE AFFECTIONATE PUPPY – These puppies are friendly and eager to please. They learn new things rather quickly and are quite easy to train. Outgoing and self-confident, they are a wonderful choice for families with children. They tend to form extraordinarily strong bonds quickly with their humans. They generally get along well with other dogs and animals and are potentially more accepting of other pets than other personality types. These dogs are happiest near their companions.

THE CALM PUPPY – More submissive than others, the calm puppy is typically happy to be a follower. Such puppies can be quite affectionate. These dogs are eager to please but sometimes require more work to motivate during training. They are mostly friendly and get along well with other dogs and animals, but they can be prone to separation anxiety when left alone.

THE FEARFUL PUPPY – Highly submissive dogs, these puppies can be quite shy and timid at times and are easily scared or intimidated. They lack self-confidence and can be quite sensitive. These dogs do best when they have a calm and quiet owner who has compassion and patience. Loud noises, punishment and even light corrections may be too much for these dogs to handle. A reputable Whoodle breeder should not have any fearful puppies in a healthy litter. Fearful puppies may be a red flag that something is wrong.

Tips for Adopting a Whoodle

If you decide to adopt a Whoodle instead of purchasing from a breeder, there are a number of resources available to you. The internet is a great place to begin your search for local Whoodle Rescues. Whoodles may even be found right in your own local animal shelter. Call or visit these places and let them know what you are looking for. If they do not currently have a Whoodle ready for adoption, they may be willing to contact you if one comes into their facility.

The Difference Between Animal Shelters and Rescues

In the United States, there are three different classifications for pet and animal rescues: municipal shelters, no-kill shelters and non-profit rescue organizations. It is important to know the differences and the benefits of each to help you better prepare in the search for your Whoodle.

MUNICIPAL SHELTERS – These shelters, run and funded by local governments, take in strays, abandoned animals, and animals surrendered by their owners. The animals there have a limited time to be adopted and are usually euthanized due to lack of space.

These government-run shelters house their animals on-site in a kennel-like environment. Most of them have veterinarians on staff that supply basic medical care as well as spay and neuter operations. They have paid staff supplemented by volunteers who help care for the dogs and clean the facility. Adoption fees are typically low at these places. Almost all require an animal to be spayed or neutered before it is adopted.

Shelters are a great option for finding local pets in need of a home. These facilities are almost always fighting an overpopulation problem. If you adopt from a shelter, be aware that the stressful environment can cause a dog to act fearful or aggressive, even if that is not its true personality. This is known as "kennel syndrome." Ask if your shelter allows trial periods where you can take the dog home for a few days to see if he is a good match for your family. This will enable you to see him outside of the high-stress environment of the kennel.

NO-KILL SHELTERS – These are private organizations that will not euthanize a healthy and adoptable animal. They have a limited intake policy and end up turning many animals away because they do not have the space to house them.

Dogs are often kept in such shelters for an extended time; months and sometimes even years go by before they are adopted. Foster homes are often used in these situations to allow the dog an opportunity to live in a home-like environment. Many times, this can help a troubled dog adjust and become more adoptable.

NON-PROFIT RESCUE ORGANIZATIONS – These organizations are mostly run and operated by volunteers. They utilize foster houses to save as many animals as possible. They do not euthanize animals.

Typically, privately funded or dependent on donations, many rescue groups are breed-specific and dedicated to saving one specific dog type, such as Whoodles. Rescues often offer the same medical care and spay and neuter services as municipal shelters, but only a few have a veterinarian on staff. These rescues often pay full price for veterinary services, which becomes a significant expense.

Most rescue groups rely heavily on foster families. Some may not have a physical facility at all but instead maintain a website with information about their available and adoptable dogs. Because the dog lives with a foster family, more is known about the dog's history and personality, making it easier to find a compatible home.

Due to their higher costs, rescues usually have much higher adoption fees than shelters do. They also have much stricter adoption guidelines and policies, and some even require a home inspection before approval. Much like with a typical breeder, many have policies in place that require adopters to return the dog to the rescue if they can no longer keep the animal.

Rescues usually maintain contact with adopters for 3 to 6 months after adoptions take place. During this time, they may do another home inspection to ensure things are going well and that the dog is happy and healthy.

Keep in mind, dogs that find their way into rescue facilities often have experienced some kind of trauma. Sometimes they come with significant health issues, social issues, or even behavioral problems. Make sure you are prepared to handle the problems that may arise from a rescued dog so that you and your adopted Whoodle can have the best life together possible.

CHAPTER 3
Preparing for Your Whoodle

Before bringing home your Whoodle, be sure to prepare your home and your family. Puppy pick-up day is exciting for everyone but there is nothing worse than getting your new pup home then realizing you weren't quite ready. Prepare for your Whoodle beforehand and the first few days with your new pup will go much smoother!

Preparing Children

If you are bringing your puppy home to a house with no children or other pets, the transition should be relatively easy. However, if you have children or other pets, you should make preparations to allow everyone time to adjust.

Teach children proper handling of your Whoodle pup before the dog comes home. Show children how to safely hold, pick up, and pet your puppy. A small child can harm a puppy unintentionally by trying to show affection in a manner that is too rough. Careful supervision should always be maintained with small children and dogs for the safety of all parties.

Remind children of new puppy basics, such as a puppy's love of chewing. Teach kids to pick up their possessions at all times and never leave them unattended with

FUN FACT
How Popular Are They?

Whoodles are a relatively new hybrid breed, which means that a popularity ranking can't accurately tell us how desirable these dogs are. Dogell, a polling website dedicated to providing statistics about dogs, ranked Whoodles 586th most popular out of 623 breeds in the United States as of 2020. As Whoodles become more prevalent, their popularity will likely grow.

your Whoodle. A mistake may result in a beloved stuffed animal being reduced to shreds.

Consider introducing older children to dog-care chores. Allow them to help in all aspects of care, such as feeding, brushing, and exercising your dog. This will help the dog bond with the kids and it will teach them a great deal of responsibility when they come to realize this little life is depending on them for care.

Photo Courtesy of Catherine Bailey

Preparing Pets

When it comes to introducing current pets to the idea of a new puppy, things may get a little more complicated. Whoodles in general are friendly, especially when you introduce them to other pets at an early age, but they do have a natural instinct to chase small animals. Take precautions when introducing a Whoodle to smaller pets.

If you have pets already, warm them up to the idea of a new puppy before the introduction. Discuss this transition with your chosen breeder and see if they will allow you to pick up a blanket or a toy with the new puppy's scent on it. Introduce the blanket or toy to your current dog or dogs and allow them to become accustomed to the smell of another puppy in the house.

When you pick up your Whoodle puppy, have someone help you with the first introduction. If possible, let your dogs meet your new pup in a neutral area where your current pets will be less likely to be territorial. Because your puppy's immune system is not fully developed, don't take him or her to a park or another public place. Instead, let the dogs meet briefly outside of the house in a less frequented area. Keep your dogs leashed but give them a bit of slack so they can greet the puppy. Closely watch all parties during the introduction to ensure the safety of your new puppy.

Photo Courtesy of Lisa Zarin

Keep the first meeting brief then separate your dogs from the new puppy so they do not overwhelm each other. After you see how the dogs react to each other, you can slowly allow them to spend more time together until they are completely acclimated.

If the dog you are introducing to your new pup is advanced in age, be extra cautious. Your older dog may be more receptive and easygoing about the new arrival or he may become stressed by the endless energy of your new Whoodle. Take your dog's cues and respect his place in the household. Give him plenty of space and time to help him adjust.

If you are introducing your Whoodle to a resident cat, it's

important to keep both your cat and your puppy safe by maintaining control of your puppy. Keeping one animal contained by a crate or another barrier may be useful at first. Allow the animals short, controlled interactions at quiet moments of the day until they are both calm around each other. Your cat should always be able to escape to a place only he can get to. This may be a place off the ground, such as a cat tree or even a favorite spot on the furniture where your dog cannot reach.

A new puppy is exciting and can become the center of attention for a while. Remember to show your other pets some extra attention so they know that they are still important members of the family.

Puppy-Proofing Your Home Indoors

There are many ordinary things in your home that could prove dangerous to your new puppy. As such, one of the first things you should do in preparation for your new Whoodle is to puppy-proof your home.

TUCK AWAY OR REMOVE ANY ELECTRICAL CORDS WITHIN THE PUPPY'S REACH. Puppies are curious little creatures who love to explore, oftentimes with their mouths. If you cannot remove all cords from your puppy's reach, you may want to invest in some cord protectors. These cord wraps usually come infused with bitter flavors to help deter your Whoodle from chewing them. If you find you have a particularly stubborn chewer, you can spritz the cords with hot pepper or bitter apple spray to ensure the dog will not find the cord appealing anymore.

INVEST IN FULLY ENCLOSED TRASH CANS IF YOU DO NOT HAVE THEM ALREADY. Keeping the kitchen trash out of reach may be a no-brainer, but even the smaller trash cans around your bathrooms and office are tempting toys for an energetic and curious Whoodle. Sometimes a used cotton swab or a wad of paper is just too irresistible not to chew up.

LOCK AWAY ALL DRUGS, CHEMICALS, AND CLEANING SUPPLIES. If you tend to keep any medications in an area that your puppy may be able to reach, be sure to move those to a higher location, such as a dedicated, locked medicine cabinet. As mentioned above, puppies explore everything with their mouths, and snatching a bottle or box of medication off the sofa table could prove to be fatal for your new puppy.

ALSO, MOVE ANY CHEMICALS, CLEANING SUPPLIES, DISH PODS, OR LAUNDRY DETERGENTS INTO AN ENCLOSED AREA, OUT OF REACH OF YOUR PUPPY. This includes any rat bait or poisons that your new puppy may find enticing.

Even if these items are in an area of the house where your puppy will not be allowed, it only takes one escape for your new Whoodle to encounter something detrimental.

WATCH OUT FOR POISONOUS HOUSE PLANTS. House plants may seem innocent, but some are poisonous and can cause serious issues for a nibbling puppy. Some common houseplants that are potentially dangerous for your new puppy are the corn plant, sago palm, aloe, and jade plant. To find a complete list of common plants which are poisonous to dogs, visit the ASPCA website.

BEWARE OF XYLITOL. This sweetener can be found in almost anything but is commonly found in chewing gum, mints, candies, toothpaste, and even peanut butter. Xylitol is highly toxic to dogs and can cause dangerously low blood sugar levels, resulting in weakness, seizures, trembling, or even death. When dogs consume very high levels of xylitol, it may cause necrosis of the liver, which often leads to death.

Be sure to keep all purses and bags which may contain gum, candies, or toothpaste out of reach of your puppy at all times. Have a designated area for guests' bags so that they are not accidentally left within reach. Also, check all food

Photo Courtesy of Dria Lobosco

labels for xylitol. Peanut butter is often recommended to give a dog medication but be sure to check that your peanut butter does not contain xylitol first.

KEEP THE BATTERIES AWAY. While you probably don't have random batteries lying around on the floor, you may have remotes or small electronic toys. If your puppy is able to get hold of a battery-operated remote or toy, he can chew them to expose the battery. Small button cell batteries are the most dangerous as they are small enough for your puppy to swallow. Swallowing a battery is a serious, life-threatening issue and can cause internal burns. Call the nearest emergency vet immediately if you suspect your puppy may have swallowed a battery.

PUT AWAY CHILDREN'S TOYS. Children's toys are often made up of small pieces that are a choking hazard to your dog. Be especially careful with toys that contain magnets inside, as these pose an extra risk of internal damage when more than one is consumed.

KEEP TOILETS CLOSED. Many people use automatically refreshing toilet bowl cleaners attached to the bowl of their toilet. These can pose risks to a thirsty pup. Remove chemical cleaners from your toilet bowl, or make sure you always keep the lid down and the bathroom door closed.

REMOVE AREA RUGS. While not necessarily dangerous, an area rug may become the prime target for potty accidents or could even be chewed up with those sharp little puppy teeth. It is best to simply remove rugs until your Whoodle is trained and can be trusted.

SET UP PUPPY GATES. After you have puppy-proofed your entire house, designate a safe, common area of the house for your puppy to stay. Use puppy gates to block any doorways or staircases so that it will be easier for you to keep a close eye on your new Whoodle.

Puppy-Proofing Your Home Outdoors

Whoodles are highly energetic and will benefit from an outdoor space to expend some of that energy. It is important to keep any outdoor area you have as a dog-friendly zone with plenty of shade with water readily available.

Start preparing your outdoor space ahead of time by removing all chemical products from the area, including the garage. Any weed or pest killer, fertilizers, antifreeze, or other similar products should be placed beyond the dog's reach.

If you plan to leave your Whoodle outside unattended for any amount of time, you will need to be sure the yard is secure. Check all fencing to be sure there are no gaps between the fence and the ground. Make sure all gates latch completely and there is no way for your dog to escape. The desire to "escape" can be strong within this crossbreed, as the Terrier in them possesses a strong desire to chase anything they see on the other side.

Your fencing should always be secure, with no gaps at the bottom, so a playful Whoodle is not lured away by a noise or a passerby across the street. Always be sure your dog is wearing his collar and tags before allowing him outside for any amount of time. While not known for digging, just like any dog, the Whoodle may be able to dig under the fence if there is something enticing him on the other side, especially if he is bored or has excess energy. Prevent this by placing your fence on a concrete base or by lining the fence with stones or pavers. The fence should also be at least 6 feet high to prevent him from jumping over.

Some people without physical fences try to use wireless electric fences. This is where the dog wears a transponder around his neck and is given a small shock if he tries to cross the invisible fence line. While these fences seem great in theory, they are only about 70% effective in keeping a dog in. An energetic Whoodle may be able to break right through that invisible plane.

Photo Courtesy of Annelies Morsink

Whoodles are generally good swimmers, but a backyard pool can easily become a danger without supervision. It's good practice to keep your pool fenced off or somehow separated from your dog so your Whoodle does not accidentally get himself into a situation when you are not there to help.

Just like with indoor plants, some outdoor plants and flowers are poisonous to your dog. Check the ASPCA website's list against any plants you may have in your garden and replace them with a safe alternative.

Stories from a Whoodle Owner

Willow

Country Dog or City Dog

Willow typically spends weekdays in New York City and weekends at our house in Ulster County, New York. Whoodles are known to be high-energy and require a lot of exercise and stimulation, so I was determined to give her a life that suits her breed.

Willow adjusted easily to her dual lifestyle and is happy no matter where she is. In the city, where she lives in a third-floor apartment, she loves going on walks and to the local dog run, particularly because she meets and plays with lots of other dogs and people along the way. The noises of the city and the concrete sidewalks don't bother her at all. Indoors, when she's not chewing on a bone or asking to be chased around the living room, she is content to doze off in her crate, at my feet, on top of the sofa or sprawled out in the shower stall where it's cool. She has five or six places she calls her own. I recently got her a staircase so she can climb up to one of the windows and look out to the street below.

Willow becomes a different dog in the country, where she is truly in her element. She emits sounds of joy when we pull into our driveway. She loves to run on grass or snow, dig in dirt, follow every scent and go on hikes with amazing stamina. She spends hours on the deck just looking at and listening to the sights and sounds of the country - birds, chipmunks, insects, trees rustling in the wind. One of her favorite activities is rolling sideways down a grassy slope - it almost looks like she is laughing.

So no matter where you live, your Whoodle is likely to be happy and willing to adjust as long as he or she gets lots of activity and stimulation

Supplies to Purchase Before You Bring Your Whoodle Home

Getting ready for a new dog can be overwhelming. There is so much information to learn and so many preparations to be made around the house. Gathering all the supplies you need before you bring your Whoodle home will make the first few days much easier for you and your puppy. Gather the following essentials and you will have all you need for the day you bring your dog home.

FOOD AND WATER BOWL – Food and water bowls come in many shapes, colors and sizes. They can be made from ceramic, stainless steel or plastic. When choosing a bowl set for your new puppy, there are a few things to consider. Plastic bowls may come in fun colors and patterns, but they are lightweight and easy to tip over and many puppies think they are fun to chew on. They are also more difficult to clean when they become scratched or damaged.

Ceramic bowls are heavier, less likely to be tipped over, and are easier to clean than plastic. They are breakable, though, so if your puppy does manage to knock a bowl over, it is likely to chip.

Stainless-steel bowls are both easy to clean and unbreakable, so even if a bowl is knocked over and kicked around, it won't be easily damaged. Bowls with wide rubber or silicone bases help to stop sliding and prevent tipping.

Another option you will find in a pet store is an elevated bowl set. These bowls are set up off the floor so that your dog does not have to bend over as far to eat. They were created to try to help prevent the issue of bloat in larger dogs, however, some studies have shown that elevated feeders can potentially contribute to bloat. Luckily, Whoodles are not particularly prone to this issue.

Most experts say an elevated feeder is unnecessary and potentially problematic. If you are adopting a dog that has neck or mobility issues, then an elevated dog feeder would be something to discuss with your veterinarian as an option.

If your Whoodle is a vigorous eater, you may want to invest in a slow feeder bowl. These bowls have obstacles in the middle to keep your dog from scarfing his food down too quickly, which may lead to vomiting.

COLLAR, TAGS, AND LEASH – One of the first things you will want to do when you get your new puppy is put on his or her collar with identification tags. These tags can be made at any local pet store or you can order one from an online retailer. It is best to always have your pet's name, your current address and your phone number on the tag.

This is meant to help a stranger return your dog in the event he ever gets loose. You can even add a little note that says, "Please Call My Family," which may encourage someone to contact you. If the sound of the tags rubbing on each other is bothersome, get a rubber protector to put around it and eliminate the noise.

Your dog should always wear a collar for identification purposes, but you may want to invest in a harness for walks and leash time. This will help you to better control your Whoodle without harming his neck while leash training him.

While retractable leashes can offer your dog greater freedom on a walk, they can often cause more issues with a dog still in training. Your dog may learn that pulling is okay because the retractable leash gives him the freedom to do so. Begin with a standard leash until your Whoodle learns proper leash etiquette. Standard leashes come in many different materials. Nylon is easy to clean and relatively cheap at a pet store. Leather or rope leashes may also be a good option if you are looking for something more comfortable to hold.

FOOD – Your breeder should send a small amount of food home with your puppy to get you through the first few days. It's best to continue feeding the same brand of food as it is probably high-quality and will save your puppy any intestinal upset from switching. If you do wish to change foods, talk with your breeder about how to do it properly. Switch the pup's food gradually by mixing in his current food with the new food over a period of a few days to prevent intestinal upset.

PUPPY-SAFE TOYS – Your puppy will have lots of energy and very sharp teeth. In order to save your belongings from becoming victim to those sharp teeth, you will want to have at least four or five different dog toys for your puppy to choose from. Before bringing him home, get at least one plush toy, one rubber toy or bone, one rope, and one ball. Buy toys with different squeaker sounds and textures to see which one your puppy will love the most. You may find that plush toys do not last long before being ripped to shreds, or you may find that your new puppy loves carrying that stuffed hippo all over the house.

Though they may be small, the puppy teeth of a Whoodle can still cause serious damage, so don't take them lightly!

Some pet stores also sell plush toys with warmers you can use to comfort your Whoodle pup on his first few nights alone. These toys simulate the feeling of another pup and will help to soothe separation anxiety from his litter. Be sure to take the toy away when it's not in use so it isn't destroyed during play time!

GROOMING BRUSH – As a puppy, your Whoodle will not need the brushing his future coat will eventually demand, as his coat will change in texture. But it is a good idea to get him used to the brush right from the start to avoid any anxiety later. Start with a small, basic medium-bristle brush. Additional information on grooming will be provided in Chapter 12.

PUPPY TRAINING TREATS – It is essential to have a safe bag of treats to help with potty training and teaching basic commands. Look for soft treats that are healthy and natural. Be sure that they contain no animal by-products, are grain-free, and have absolutely no artificial flavors, colors or preservatives.

CRATE AND PAD – Your puppy will need somewhere safe to stay while you are gone or when you cannot keep a close eye on him, such as at night. Invest in a quality crate and pad that will accommodate your Whoodle at his full, adult size. Establish it as a safe place early on in the training process. Buy a washable crate pad that has minimal stuffing because chances are, it will be chewed on at some point. More specifics on crates and crate training can be found in Chapter 5.

PUPPY GATE OR PLAYPEN – Do not give your new puppy full range of the house right away. Unless your space allows you to keep your puppy contained in a centralized location, you will probably want to purchase a puppy gate or playpen. The idea is to give your young Whoodle his own designated "safe space" where he can play without constant supervision.

A gate that blocks a doorway is a good way to keep your puppy from venturing down a hall, up the stairs, or into a room that is off-limits. But a gate still allows the puppy access to furniture and other things, which could potentially get chewed up. A playpen allows much more flexibility, as you can move it around wherever inside or outside of the house you will be. A playpen also keeps any furniture from becoming damaged by those razor-sharp puppy teeth.

Choosing the Right Veterinarian

It is important to know where you will take your dog for veterinary care before you bring the dog home. Find a vet you trust beforehand so you are prepared from day one to provide your Whoodle with the best care possible.

When searching for the perfect veterinarian for your new Whoodle, you may be tempted to go online and read reviews. Beware that not all reviews are an accurate depiction of an establishment. Instead, start with word of mouth. Ask fellow dog owners which vet they prefer and which ones they would avoid. Make a list of the most favorable vets and start with those.

Next, eliminate some vets from your list based on location. In an emergency, you will want to have chosen a vet that is nearby. If there are any clinics on your list that you feel are too far in the event of a crisis, cross them off.

Call all the remaining clinics on your list and inquire about their prices. You can get a good comparison by asking what they charge for a round of shots, a spay or neuter, and an X-ray. Make notes of what each clinic charges and how they accept payment. Do they demand it all upfront or do they offer payment plans? Also make note of the friendliness of the office staff when you call. Did they offer the information willingly or seem put out? You don't want to commit to a vet clinic with unhelpful office staff. That could make any visit an unpleasant experience.

Also consider convenience factors. Check out the website to get a sense of the practice and to get a complete list of services. Call the office and notice how easy or hard it is to get an appointment. When you call, are you put on hold or is there an answering machine? How is their follow-up if you leave a message?

After all of the above steps, if you still haven't decided, call each clinic and ask to make an appointment to visit in person. While on your visits, ask the staff or the vet if they have any other Whoodles as patients or have experience with the breed. You will likely find that one of the offices is a better fit for you and your puppy than the others and your decision will then be easy. It is important to trust your veterinarian and feel comfortable in their clinic so don't settle on a vet without taking all the necessary steps.

Dangerous Things Your Dog Might Eat

Although feeding your dog food from the table is not recommended, it is often difficult to resist that adorably fluffy face and those begging eyes looking up at you while you eat. If you do get the urge to toss your pup a little treat, be aware of what he can and cannot have. There are a number of foods that are perfectly healthy for humans, but can cause illness or toxicity in dogs.

Stories from a Whoodle Owner

Puberty

Flynn's breeder, like most breeders with experience and a firm business plan, required documented proof that Flynn had to be neutered by his first birthday. Flynn's vet told us that current veterinary recommendations are that owners wait as long as possible, but certainly until the first year, before neutering a pup. We committed to following our vet's recommendations, and penciled in to the calendar surgery just prior to his birthday.

Then, puberty happened (it does, pretty predictably). Flynn's beloved playmate Izzie, who was spayed when Flynn was just four months old, was confused and disappointed by her buddie's strange behavior, and his new "play" routines. His other regular playmate Nuka, as an older, dominant female, told him in no uncertain terms not to come anywhere near her with such ideas.

At age 10 ½ months, we caved, and reached out to the vet about Flynn's extra equipment, begging that in order to manage his social life, we really needed to cut this developing problem off as soon as possible, rather than waiting for his first birthday.

Most Europeans assume that they will train their (male) dogs to show restraint and behave appropriately regardless of their social environment, but we certainly were not ready for that kind of challenge. Fortunately, our vet agreed, and soon we once again had a happy puppy who just wanted to play with his best friend.

CHOCOLATE – A crowd favorite among humans, chocolate can cause major issues for your loving Whoodle. Chocolate contains methylxanthine, which is a stimulant that can stop a dog's metabolic process. Methylxanthines are found in especially high amounts in pure dark chocolate and baker's chocolate. Too much methylxanthine causes seizures and irregular heart function, which can lead to death.

XYLITOL – As discussed earlier, xylitol is particularly dangerous to dogs as it does not take much to cause a dangerous or deadly reaction. Vomiting is typically the initial symptom of xylitol poisoning. If you suspect there is a chance your dog has ingested even a small amount of xylitol, call the veterinarian immediately because time is critical.

RAW OR COOKED BONES – Raw or cooked bones are a choking hazard. The bones can break or splinter and become lodged or, worse, puncture your Whoodle's digestive tract. This is especially true with cooked bones of any kind, as they become dry and brittle. Pork and poultry bones are especially dangerous as they are more likely to splinter and cause issues.

Though controversial, some veterinarians say that raw bones of the right variety can provide healthy nutrients and help prevent tartar and plaque build-up in the mouth. These bones are recommended only under close supervision and only for a few minutes at a time. Keep the bone in the refrigerator for a maximum of four days before discarding it. If the bone is breaking or if your dog seems to be swallowing any pieces, get rid of the bone immediately. If you prefer to skip the risk, look for bones in the pet store that are meant to withstand the chewing power of a Whoodle.

Other foods that may cause gastrointestinal upset or worse for your dog are grapes and raisins, certain nuts including macadamia nuts, avocados, apple cores, seeds, and anything in the allium family, including onions and garlic. This is not a comprehensive list, so it is best to check with your veterinarian before giving anything from your plate to your dog.

CHAPTER 4

Bringing Home Your Whoodle

There is nothing more exciting than the day you get to pick up your new Whoodle from the breeder! You've done your research, prepared your home and yard, purchased all the needed supplies, and now all that's left is to bring your puppy home. You may find yourself a bit anxious, wondering how everything will go, but if you follow the tips below, pick-up day should be fun, exciting and trouble free.

Photo Courtesy of Debra Roberts

Picking Up Your Whoodle

When you arrive at the facility for pick-up day, your breeder should have the puppy ready to go in a designated pick-up area. The puppy may be in a pen playing with other puppies that are leaving on the same day. Try not to let the sight of your new Whoodle distract you from hearing the important information your breeder will give you.

Make sure you have a collar or a harness that fits your tiny new pup and a leash. If the weather is cold, you may want to bring a sweater or a blanket for your Whoodle.

Before you leave, your breeder will give you detailed information on your pup's vet records, current shots, future shots, and dewormings. They should remind you of any stipulations of the health guarantee and advise you on a feeding schedule. All of this information as well as breed-specific care tips should be neatly presented in a packet of some sort.

Sometimes a breeder will allow you to take a small blanket or toy home with your dog so that the smell of his litter can comfort him during the transition. It may be beneficial to ask ahead of time if this is an option in order to know if you need to provide the blanket before pick-up day.

Some breeders even allow you to bring a T-shirt or a blanket to your pup before pick-up day so he can become familiar with your scent ahead of time, too.

The Ride Home

Depending on how far you have to travel to pick up your puppy, you will want to plan accordingly. Motion sickness and vomiting is common on the ride home, so you might request that the breeder withhold food for that morning. Regardless of how long the trip is, you will want to be sure to take a bowl and a bottle of water for your puppy in the case of an unexpected delay, such as a flat tire.

Don't give in to the temptation to let the puppy ride home in your lap as this is dangerous. In the event of a crash, the puppy can be killed by the airbag or become a projectile. Even braking too hard can cause injury to an unsecured puppy.

Some people like to take a crate and let the puppy ride home that way. If you plan to transport the puppy in a crate, place only towels in the bottom of the crate so that the crate pad is not soiled on the trip. Also, take care to drive smoothly, so you do not jostle your puppy more than necessary.

Not all crates will withstand the force of a crash, though, and some can even become more dangerous for your dog in the event of a collision. When not properly secured to the vehicle, the crate can become a projectile, injuring your puppy and possibly other passengers in the car. Visit the Center for Pet Safety (CPS) website for a list of tested and approved travel crates.

Photo Courtesy of Cabrina Little

If you are thinking of buying a harness for your dog to use in the car, know that they are not all created equally. The Center for Pet Safety performed a Harness Crashworthiness Study in 2013, and results showed that only one of eleven brands tested performed at the level advertised. Some were even deemed "catastrophic failures." Do diligent research on each brand before making your decision, so you can be sure you get a safe one.

Whether you choose to put your puppy in a crate or in harness, make sure he's securely restrained for the duration of the car ride.

Before beginning the journey home, allow your Whoodle to use the restroom on a patch of grass and praise him when he does. The ride home should be a positive experience for all and can be a great bonding opportunity for you and your puppy. Enjoy those first moments together as a new family!

Pet Transportation Services

If you cannot travel to pick up your new Whoodle pup directly, you may need to hire a pet transportation service to help you get your dog home safely. These services can be very pricey and are typically used for long distance or international moves. If you do choose to go this route, make sure your chosen company is reputable and a member of the International Pet and Animal Transportation Association (IPATA).

Photo Courtesy of Jana Losee

These companies will take care of all the logistics of both air and ground travel and provide your dog with a safe and stressless journey to you. Services and perks vary by company so make sure you do your research to know exactly what care your pup will receive.

The First Night

If possible, you may want to take a few days off work to be home with your new pup as you get into a routine. For the first night home, many people choose to let the puppy sleep in a crate in their room. You could also put it in a separate room, as long as you can hear the puppy when he needs to go outside to relieve himself. Try to pick a designated area and stick with it so that you and your new Whoodle can quickly get accustomed to his new spot.

Before bed, take your puppy outside and wait for him to relieve himself. If the puppy does not go, wait ten minutes, then try again. Repeat this process for however long it takes your puppy to go then put him into the crate for bed with his special blanket or toy from the breeder. It will be helpful for nighttime potty runs if you keep the crate by your bed.

The first night home can be upsetting for both you and your puppy as this will be his first time away from his litter. There will probably be a lot of whining and crying for the first few nights and that is perfectly normal. Although it will be tempting to pull your puppy out of the crate and let him sleep with you, it would be best for everyone if you allow your Whoodle to self-soothe.

Remember that your puppy will probably need to be taken outside to relieve himself several times a night. When your puppy wakes you in the night, it is best to take him outside, then immediately return him to the crate to sleep. If he cries going back into the crate, let him self-soothe. This will teach him that nighttime is for sleeping and not for playing.

If your puppy is having a difficult time sleeping in the crate or keeps you awake with his crying, try talking to your puppy or rubbing his head through the crate to help calm him. You always want to make your puppy feel loved and secure, even as you allow him to self-soothe. Bonds you form with each other in the early days will last throughout your dog's lifetime.

FUN FACT
Dog Lovers of *Glee*

Glee star Romy Rosemont, who played Carole Hudson in the popular TV show, said in an interview with Modern Dog magazine that if she were a dog, she would be a Whoodle. "The name just makes me laugh," Rosemont said, "I have the energy of a Wheaten and the hair of a Poodle. These dogs are known to be energetic and playful; they're people-oriented and very eager to please. They have a strong work drive but tend to get bored easily and are good at finding trouble. Did someone just describe me?" Rosemont owns two dogs named Purdy and Bazooka Joe, neither of which is a Whoodle.

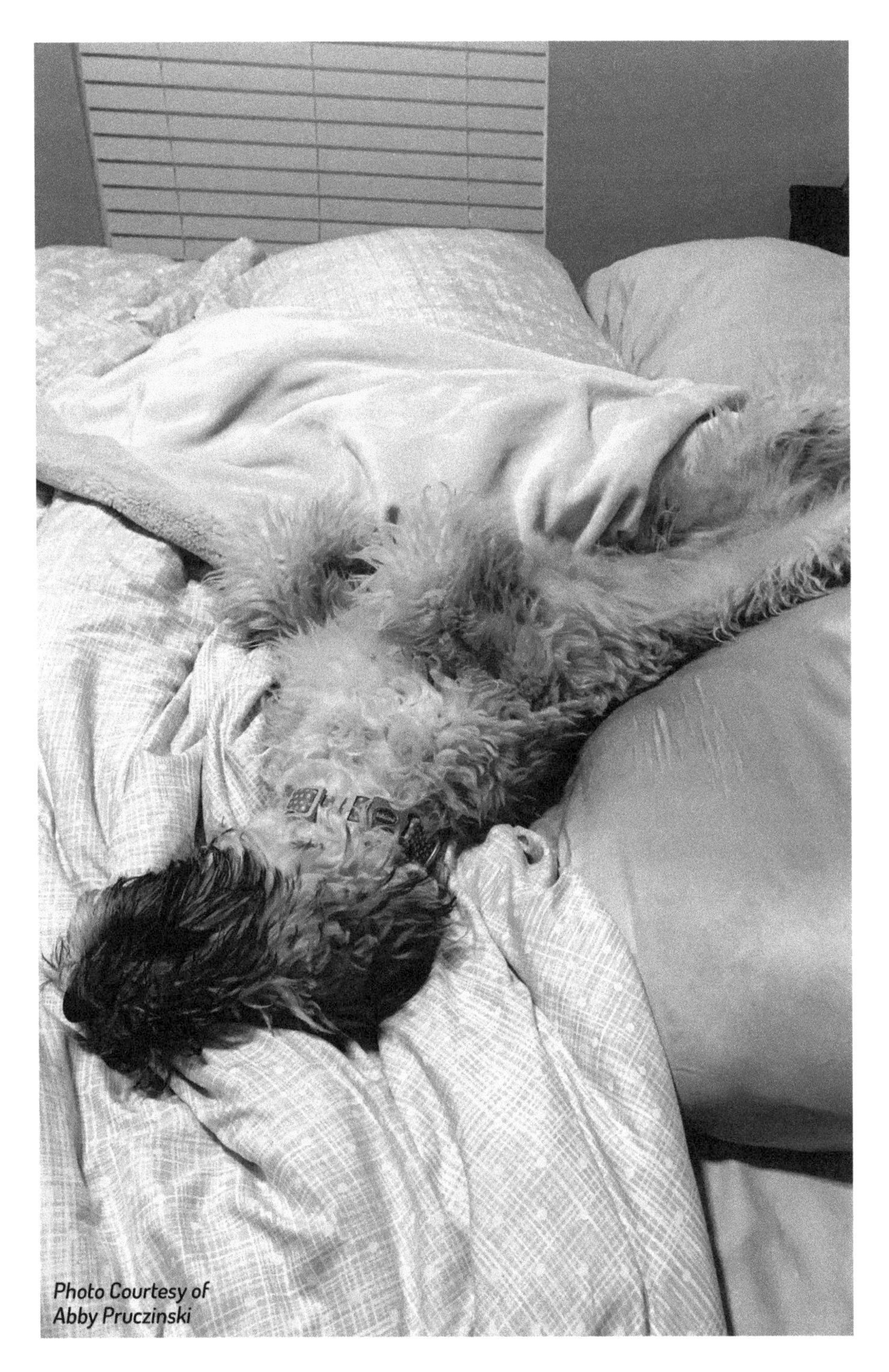

Photo Courtesy of
Abby Pruczinski

After a few nights, the bedtime whining should ease up and eventually stop, and your puppy will come to find his crate a cozy place to sleep. As you and your Whoodle puppy adjust to life with each other, routines will form, and things will get much easier.

The First Vet Visit

Some breeders' contracts stipulate that you must take your puppy to the vet within a few days for a checkup. If this is the case, you will want to call and make an appointment with your chosen vet before you pick up your puppy. Be sure to take all records given to you by the breeder for the vet to include in your Whoodle's file. Even if the breeder doesn't require this first vet visit, it is a good idea to take your pup anyway.

The first appointment will typically be a general checkup to make sure your pup is healthy. Your puppy will be weighed and the vet will examine eyes, ears, nose, heart and lungs. They will look at your dog's skin and coat condition and examine his teeth and mouth. They may take a stool sample to check for parasites. If it is time for your puppy's next round of shots, he will get them at this appointment.

The first vet appointment should be relatively quick and easy. Ask your vet any questions you may have about feeding or caring for your new puppy. If you have made a list of questions, pull it out so you don't forget anything and make sure you get thorough answers.

Many puppies have intestinal parasites that can cause diarrhea. Your breeder should advise you on a de-wormer to administer. If you are concerned about this, talk to your vet.

Parvovirus

Parvo is a serious and life-threatening infection for your pup. This disease is caused by the canine parvovirus and is highly contagious. It can be transmitted through direct contact with a sick dog or by indirect contact via a contaminated surface.

This disease is important for city dwellers to take seriously because it can be very dangerous for a puppy to sniff infected urine or poop. Many vets recommend that puppies in the city don't leave the home or apartment until it's had all vaccinations at 15 weeks, which means 7 weeks of home confinement. Most new owners who live in the city are surprised by this, because it means you can't start housebreaking your puppy or allow it to play safely during these important, formative weeks.

It is also recommended that all visitors remove their shoes at the front door so they don't bring in any infections. And whether the puppy is a city or country dweller, it should never go to the dog park or run until it has had all its shots.

Your first days with your new puppy will probably be a combination of wonderful and frustrating. You may get a little less sleep than normal, but the bond you and your puppy are creating during this time will be well worth the work you are putting in now, no matter how many accidents you have to clean up along the way.

Stories from a Whoodle Owner

Willow

Relationships from a Whoodle's Perspective

I picked Willow up from the breeder when she was exactly eight weeks old. She bonded with me immediately, which is one of the greatest advantages of getting a new pup at that specific age. I quickly became her new "mom." She started following me everywhere.

Because my vet recommended keeping her away from other dogs until she had her final round of vaccinations at 15 weeks, she would have to be quarantined in my apartment in New York City. But instead of heading there, I chose to take her to my cabin upstate, where the risk of infectious diseases was much smaller and where she could spend some time outdoors. We had a wonderful time together as she got used to her new life and we strengthened the bond between us.

But when I brought her back to the city a week later, she was utterly confused when she met my husband. Who was he? If I was the mom, he had to be a litter mate! And so, Willow's relationship with him became just that. While she listened to me, and came to me for instruction and care, my husband became her playmate. To this day, she plays with him in just the same way she roughhouses with other dogs and puppies, with full-body slams, playful bites, grunts and growls. She never does this with me.

The Cost of Ownership

Many dog owners underestimate how expensive it is to own and properly care for a dog, often taking only the initial purchase price into consideration. While this is definitely a factor, there are a number of other expenses that need to be considered as well. Your Whoodle is completely dependent on you for everything, so it's important to be prepared for all of the responsibilities and financial requirements that come with owning a dog.

The Whoodle is what some would call a "Designer Dog," and people will pay significant amounts of money to acquire one, despite the breed not being recognized by the American Kennel Club. Depending on location, Whoodle puppies will sell anywhere from $1,000 to $4,000.

Purchase price is not the only cost to consider. The first year of a dog's life can be expensive. When you consider the supplies you will need to buy, veterinary visits and training classes, the cost can really add up. Most puppies come with their first round of shots but you will need to be sure they get the rest from a vet. It is also important to remember, unless you plan to breed your Whoodle, that the cost of a spay or neuter can vary depending on location but generally costs from $75 to $250 or more, depending on cost of living in your area.

Because Whoodles can vary in sizes, they cost anywhere from $300 to $700 to feed a year. The premium dog food brands may seem expensive, but they will ultimately lead to better health and overall quality of life.

Vet bills are typically the biggest expense for dog owners. Depending on where you live, the office fee alone is about $50 and an exam can cost upwards of $100 or more. A spay or neuter operation can cost more than $200. Vaccines are relatively cheap at between $20 and $30 each, but testing for anything from heartworm to diagnostic bloodwork can cost anywhere from $20 to $250. If there is a more serious illness or injury, things can get incredibly expensive in a hurry. X-rays and ultrasounds can cost $300 to $400. Anesthesia and surgery procedures for emergencies can run into thousands of dollars.

Pet insurance can help to offset some of these costs, but it can cost an average of $500 to $600 per year. Some pet policies have deductibles which can be higher or lower based on your price. Take all of this into consideration before choosing a policy.

Also, consider the cost of boarding your Whoodle when you are away for an extended period. If you travel often and do not plan to take your dog, these costs can add up quickly. Look into local boarding facilities to find pricing for your area.

Many owners like to take their dog to a boarding facility for day care to socialize with other dogs. Some also hire walkers to provide their dogs with ample exercise while they are at work. These services can add to the cost of ownership quite a bit over the course of a year.

There can also be costs associated with living with your dog. Leasing agents and landlords usually require a pet deposit when you sign your lease and these usually run between $200 and $700.

Grooming is another expense that needs to be considered. A bath is relatively inexpensive at $20 to $40, but anything more than that can be quite costly. A full grooming, which your Whoodle will need often, can cost as much as $120 or more if you live in a high-cost area.

Training can also be an unexpected cost. If you opt to seek assistance from a professional, an hour with a private in-home trainer will cost around $100 per session, while a 6-week group class costs an average of $200 to $300.

Another factor to consider is homeowner's insurance. This will usually cover any damage done by a domestic pet to people, property or other pets. However, many renters and apartment dwellers do not have this kind of coverage, which opens them up to personal liability if their dog bites another dog and there are vet bills. People who don't want to purchase homeowner's insurance can get an umbrella policy for liability coverage.

It is wise to consider all of the potential costs of owning and raising your Whoodle before you bring him home. If you are financially able to purchase and care for a Whoodle his entire life, he will reward you with a lifetime of energetic loyalty, love and companionship.

CHAPTER 5

Being a Puppy Parent

Whether you're a seasoned veteran or a first-time puppy parent, you will undoubtedly encounter new things when you bring home your Whoodle pup. Every dog is different and comes with its own challenges. This chapter will help you understand and conquer anything you may face as a new puppy parent.

Have Realistic Expectations

Being a puppy parent is not always fun. In fact, raising a puppy is hard work and takes a lot of time and dedication. It involves getting up in the middle of the night to take your dog outside, cleaning up accidents and always keeping a watchful eye to be sure nothing is being destroyed by those sharp puppy teeth. No matter how well-mannered your particular puppy may seem, no puppy parents get by completely unscathed and many lose a pair or two of shoes along the way.

If you think raising your Whoodle will be easy, reconsider. Puppies are challenging. However, the reward you will receive after going through the challenging phases together will be a well-mannered, loyal and loving companion that will always stick by your side.

Chewing

One of the most frustrating things about caring for a puppy is the chewing. Chewing is a way for puppies to explore the world and help relieve any pain caused by incoming adult teeth. It is inevitable and unstoppable, so don't reprimand your puppy for doing what comes naturally. Instead, be sure he has plenty of safe toys or rubber bones to chew. That way, your puppy will not be tempted to chew on your favorite pair of sandals.

Photo Courtesy of Carrie Kolbin

When you catch your puppy chewing on something he or she shouldn't be, remove the item or the puppy from the situation and give him an appropriate chew toy. This positive "take and replace" technique is much more effective than punishing the puppy. Never let your puppy chew on your fingers or hands. This is a habit that is very difficult to break once established.

If you're not sure what an appropriate chew toy is, Kate Perry from Kate Perry Dog Training in New York City suggests 3-inch hollow sterilized bones, raw beef marrow bones, Kongs, Twist 'n Treat, bully sticks and Flossies. She advises to never give rawhide as it isn't digestible and can create a blockage in your dog's intestines. If you're considering giving your Whoodle real bones, refer back to Chapter 3 for more information.

If your puppy is a persistent chewer, you may want to invest in some bitter-apple spray. This is intended to deter dogs from chewing due to its bad taste.

Chewing due to teething will likely stop when your puppy's adult teeth have come in, around five to six months of age. However, some dogs chew more than others and will continue the habit into young adulthood. In either case, it's important to always have a safe and desirable chew toy available for your dog. Try some of the safe options listed above and find what appeals to your Whoodle the most.

Digging

In general, dogs dig for many reasons. Some dig out of boredom, because they're hot and want to lie in the cool dirt, or just for the fun and adventure of it. Well, if you find yourself with a spunky Whoodle that loves to get his paws into the dirt, grass or gravel, you're not alone. Whoodles are born diggers and love to get those paws moving. While digging is a natural behavior and shouldn't be punished, you should take precautions around the yard and house to keep your dog safe.

If your Whoodle is digging under a fence, try to determine the reason he may be doing this. Is he not getting enough mental stimulation? The curiosity and energetic nature of a bored Whoodle could lead him to seek out an adventure on the other side of the fence if the opportunity presents itself. Due to the breed's natural instinct to chase small animals, your Whoodle may find himself digging to hunt them down. Read more about Whoodles and safe fencing in Chapter 3.

For avid diggers, you may want to designate a "safe spot" for your dog to dig. An area in the yard away from the fence and garden, or even a box filled with sand, will allow him to safely satisfy those digging urges without the destruction that can come along with it.

If you reside in an urban area and your Whoodle is unable to dig outside, try filling a box with blankets or towels that your dog can dig in and bury things. It can be quite comical to watch your Whoodle "dig" to bury toys and treats in a box filled with blankets! This may also save your couch cushions from becoming victims.

If digging gets out of control, you may need to take a different approach. Try letting your dog outside under supervised conditions only. Allow your dog to do his business then offer him a game of fetch. If you allow your digging Whoodle to entertain himself unsupervised, you may find some sizable craters in your yard.

Stories from a Whoodle Owner

Willow

Digging is a Way of Life

Terriers were bred to dig out quarry. They also love to bury treasures for safekeeping. Willow is a born digger. When she was just 8 weeks old, I introduced her to my garden. It was April and not yet planted for the season. The soil was perfect and dig she did. She dug and dug and dug, creating a crater big enough to fit her body into, then moving on to make another one a few yards away. This is still one of her favorite activities, although she is not welcome in the garden during planting and growing season.

Willow loves to dig indoors too. She digs on rugs, sofas, beds, under tables, and inside her crate when she is given a bone, dental chew or bully stick. She'll spend minutes on end trying to hide it behind a cushion, under a pillow, or inside a heap of clothes. After she's satisfied that it's been successfully placed, she proceeds to cover it by repeatedly flicking her nose to push imaginary dirt over it. Then, maybe later in the day or whenever she's in the mood, she will retrieve it and chew to her heart's content. She clearly keeps an inventory of where all her treats are safely buried.

Barking and Growling

One of the Whoodle's desirable traits is their quiet nature. Whoodles make decent watch dogs but will only sound the alarm when something is wrong, unlike some dogs that seem to bark at anything that moves.

While Whoodles aren't avid barkers, they will still bark on occasion, depending on individual personality. This can become an issue, especially for city dwellers who have close neighbors. Some apartment or condo residents have been forced to move or rehome their dog because of barking issues and complaining neighbors. If your neighbors are objecting to your dog's barking while you are away, set up a camera so you can see how he is behaving while you are gone. This can help you become more informed to address the barking issue. If you do not have access to set up a camera on your dog, call one phone and leave it on in the room with your Whoodle when you leave. This will allow you to hear what your dog is doing after you walk out the door.

If your dog is barking to get your attention, break the habit by teaching him that making this noise doesn't work. When your Whoodle barks at you, turn away and ignore until the barking stops. Then turn back and reward the quiet with a "Yes" and a treat. Repeat this until your dog understands that barking does not get rewarded with treats or attention. You may also need to use a tool to interrupt your dog to stop the barking. This could be a squirt bottle, air spray or the noise from a squeak toy. Wait a few seconds after the barking stops and reward the same as before.

A Whoodle will be friendly to all and show no aggressive tendencies. If you're in the middle of a tug-of-war match with your new puppy, and you hear him let out a vicious growl, the puppy is usually not growling out of aggression. When puppies play, they will often display loud barking, growling, chasing and pouncing. This is natural in a puppy's development and is how he would be playing with his littermates to establish new skills and better coordination.

If you want to discourage play fighting, don't do it by punishing your puppy. These are natural behaviors that should simply be ignored. If your puppy begins to play too rough and bark and growl, stop playing immediately and walk away. Come back when the puppy settles down. If your puppy continues to play too rough, repeat the process until your puppy grasps the idea of what is and is not acceptable. This will take time but is well worth the effort.

If your dog seems truly agitated or begins nipping and biting in a way that seems defensive, schedule a trip to see the vet. Truly agitated growling and biting behavior in a previously well-mannered dog can indicate a health problem that may be causing your dog pain.

Photo Courtesy of Annelies Morsink

Separation Anxiety

Most puppies will whine or bark when left alone. This is normal behavior and will typically stop as the dog becomes accustomed to short spans of time alone. After all, your pup has just gone through a major life change by being separated from his mother and litter mates.

However, a dog with true separation anxiety will bark and pace persistently until you return. He may become destructive, chewing and clawing things out of distress. Even a housetrained dog may urinate or defecate in the house repeatedly when left alone if he suffers from separation anxiety. In extreme cases, a dog may display signs of coprophagia, a condition when a dog defecates then consumes his stool.

Dogs are pack animals and instinctually do not like to be alone. The display of anxiety stems from a primal fear of being abandoned.

It may be helpful to take your dog for a walk or play fetch with him for a while just before you leave the house. Hopefully, this will tire your dog out and he will be too exhausted to get worked up while you're gone. You can also try leaving your Whoodle with an interactive toy. Try a treat ball or a dog puzzle that will reward him with treats periodically. This may be just enough distraction to get your dog through his time alone. Make this toy or puzzle a special thing your dog only gets when he's alone. This can help positively reinforce that being on his own can be a treat.

For a dog with separation anxiety, it's important that he doesn't associate your return with overexcitement. When you return, do not immediately run to greet your dog. Ignore him for a full two minutes or until he is calm. This will help him understand that your return from being away is not a reward for him.

Crate training is especially helpful for separation anxiety. Making his kennel a safe haven for him may help ease his stress while he is left alone. By crate training him, he will become accustomed to having his own space alone while you are home with him. This will make it easier on him when he is in the kennel while you are away.

If your Whoodle is restless and noisy in the kennel, practice a "walk-by" only when he is calm. As long as he is upset, stay out of his sight. As soon as he calms down, quietly walk by his kennel without acknowledging him. This will teach him that calmness in the kennel is rewarded with your presence. Some trainers also suggest filling an empty soda can with loose change to rattle any time your pup begins to bark or whine in the kennel. When your pup quiets down, the noise stops, teaching him that his quietness is rewarded with quietness.

Photo Courtesy of Amy Alering

If the separation anxiety is severe and nothing seems to work, make an appointment with your vet to check that there is nothing else going on. They may be able to advise you on some safe ways to keep your dog calm when you have to leave the house without him.

Crate Training Basics

Dogs are not true den animals by nature, but they need a safe, quiet space to go to when they feel scared or anxious. In the wild, dogs and wolves only den when they rear puppies. These dens are usually holes dug in the ground by the mother wolf. The holes are abandoned when the puppies are old enough to travel with the pack. Although domesticated dogs' ancestors didn't spend their days in a den, that doesn't mean your new puppy won't find comfort in a "den" of his own in your house.

While crate training can be a controversial topic among dog owners, the crate is a necessary tool used to protect and secure a dog. Crate training your Whoodle makes puppy ownership easier for you and safer for your puppy. When done properly, crating your dog is an excellent tool for house-training and will set your dog up for success from the start.

When shopping for a crate, there are multiple types to choose from. These include plastic, wire, soft, and heavy-duty versions. The two main types are plastic and wire. If you plan to travel with your dog by plane, you will need to purchase a plastic crate as these are the only crates allowed for air travel.

Wire crates allow more visibility and airflow then fold flat for easy storage when not in use. Line the crate with a commercial pad or an old towel or blanket for comfort. Regardless of what type of crate you buy, get one big enough for your Whoodle when he's fully grown, otherwise you'll have to buy another one. Many come with dividers you can use to make the usable area of the crate smaller while your dog is young and gradually expand as your dog grows.

The key to successful crate training is positive reinforcement. The crate is intended to be a safe place for your dog, a place he can go for rest and comfort. Do not ever put your dog in the crate as a form of punishment. This sends the message that the crate is a bad place. You don't want your dog to view the crate as a "timeout" box or he will never retreat there willingly.

The first time you introduce your new puppy to the crate, have some training treats on hand. Secure the door of the crate to the side so it doesn't accidentally swing closed and scare your pup. Begin by placing a treat or two outside, near the door of the crate. Depending on how your dog reacts

Photo Courtesy of Bree Candee

HELPFUL TIP
Whoodles and Kids

Whoodles are a popular choice for families with children. These adorable pups have lots of energy and are known for their playfulness and friendly nature, making them the perfect addition to an active family. Children need to learn to be gentle with the family dog, but Whoodles generally have the friendly disposition needed for homes with kids and are not known to have a proclivity for biting.

to the crate, slowly place the treats closer until you can put one inside. Your puppy should voluntarily go inside the crate to get the treat.

Don't shut the door of the crate the first few times the puppy goes in. Instead, praise him and allow him to come in and out of the crate freely. After your puppy becomes comfortable with the open crate, guide him inside and gently latch the door. Give him treats from outside the crate and verbally praise him. Only leave him in there for a few moments at first and stay with him. This will help him feel comfortable. Practice this exercise the first day you get your puppy home to get him comfortable with the crate before his first night in it.

If your dog seems overly anxious in the crate, try draping a blanket over the top to block your dog's view from all but one side. This can make the crate seem more cave-like and help your pup feel more secure.

Any time you need to crate your dog, make sure to reward him with treats and a special toy. Praise him and make it a fun experience to get inside the crate. Don't leave your dog in the crate for long the first few times, with the exception of nighttime, or he may begin to get anxious and associate those feelings with the crate. Practice leaving your puppy in the crate while you're home for short increments of time, such as 30 minutes to an hour. Always immediately take your dog outside to his potty area when you let him out of the crate.

It is not reasonable for you to put your dog in a crate without first allowing him to expend his energy. Be sure to exercise your dog thoroughly beforehand. Doing this will allow him to rest and sleep in his crate while you're away, further minimizing the chances of separation anxiety.

The crate is a tool that should be used responsibly. Never leave your dog in a crate for an extended period or treat the crate like a dog-sitter. Hopefully, with proper training, your puppy will outgrow his need for the crate and will no longer need to be confined to it while you're sleeping or away. If your puppy doesn't view the crate as a place of rest and comfort, you may need to reevaluate the way you're using it.

Leaving Your Dog Home Alone

The first time you leave your Whoodle home alone can be nerve-wracking for both of you. Hopefully, you have already introduced your dog to the crate and allowed him to practice spending time alone in it. Before leaving your dog for the first time, play with your dog vigorously to wear him out or take him on a jog or a long walk. When it's time for him to go into the crate, follow the same guidelines outlined in the previous section. Reward your dog with a treat for entering the crate and give him a special "crate only" toy as an additional reward and boredom buster. Interactive treat toys like Kongs work great for this.

When you return from your first trip away, it may seem fitting to greet your puppy excitedly but refrain. You don't want to make your dog think getting out of the crate is more exciting than going in. Going in the crate should be fun and exciting but getting out should be no big deal.

When you let your dog out, open the door to the crate calmly. Remember, the crate is a safe place of rest for your dog, not a place of punishment or a place of waiting. If you let your dog out of the crate with too much excitement, you will inadvertently train him to be overexcited when the crate door opens.

Crate training takes time and effort. Some Whoodles take to it quickly and easily, while others need more time and practice. If your Whoodle does not like to be left alone, it is especially important that you don't overuse the crate. This can cause him anxiety and loneliness, leading to social and behavior issues.

Adult dogs will need to go out to relieve themselves 3 to 5 times a day and puppies will need to much more frequently. The larger your pup is, the longer he should be able to hold it, but even so, never leave your dog in the kennel so long that he has no choice but to soil it. If you intend to leave your dog home for an extended time while you work, look into daytime care for your pup.

CHAPTER 6

Potty Training Your Whoodle

Methods of Potty Training

Potty training your puppy will take a lot of time and energy. It typically takes four to six months for a dog to be fully trained, sometimes longer. The only proper way to potty train is using positive reinforcement. Never reprimand a dog and "rub his nose in it." This method does not work and is cruel punishment for a puppy that doesn't know any better.

Teach your new puppy that your home is also his, where he eats and sleeps, and instinctually he will not want to soil it. Slowly introduce your dog to small, controlled areas of your house until he views the space as his own.

Photo Courtesy of Stacey McCumiskey

This could be a playpen or a wire crate in the room with you when you first start the training. Over time, you can expand the area your dog is allowed in until, eventually, he knows that he should only relieve himself outside. A dog should never have full reign of the house until he is at least a year old.

Country Life Magazine UK published a list of the top 15 non-pedigree dogs in June 2020. The list is in no particular order, but Whoodles proudly make the list. The magazine describes these dogs as "blonde and bubbly like a young Barbara Windsor" and recommends them to "a well-turned-out dressage rider," dressage being an equestrian sport.

Take your puppy out often, about every hour, and reward him freely with verbal praise and treats. Consistently take him to the same area so he will smell his scent and know that it's time to urinate. Use a command such as "pee-pee" or "go potty" when he relieves himself so he will associate that command with the action. Make this time with your puppy calm and all about business. Do your best to ignore his attempts to play until after he's finished so that he doesn't forget the reason he went outside in the first place.

It may take 10 to 15 minutes, but when your dog relieves himself, celebrate enthusiastically and reward him with a treat and a lot of verbal praise. This will help show him that going potty outside is a positive and fun experience.

If you are having trouble with accidents at night, consider taking your dog's water away an hour before bed. If your Whoodle is thirsty, fill his bowl with ice.

For those who live in the city, some breeders suggest keeping your dog confined to your home for the first seven or so weeks after you bring your Whoodle home to prevent your young pup from coming into contact with any serious viruses such as parvo. While this may be necessary to keep your Whoodle puppy safe, it will add an extra challenge to potty training.

Utilize puppy pads for the first seven weeks until it is safe for your dog to venture out. These are small pads scented to encourage your dog to "go" there. Put these in a centralized location so your dog knows his designated area. If you need to, begin by laying out several to create a larger area for him to go. After he becomes accustomed to the pads, you can make the area smaller and use one pad at a time. While it isn't ideal, if you must keep your dog inside for a time, it can be a last resort.

Bell Training Your Whoodle

Some dog owners choose to bell train their new Whoodle pups. The theory here is to teach your dog to ring the bell, which is located on the door to the outside, whenever he needs to relieve himself. Begin this training by encouraging your dog to ring the bell with his nose. When he does, praise him and give him a training treat.

Once your dog has learned to touch the bell with his nose, incorporate the word "bell" every time he does it. Continue to praise him and give him treats for successful ringing. After your dog has learned to ring the bell on command, place the bell on the handle of the door that you take him out to relieve himself. Using the command "bell" have him practice ringing it on command while it is on the door. When he does, open the door and take him out directly to his designated "potty" spot. With some practice, your Whoodle will learn that ringing the bell means he gets to go outside to potty.

Make sure you only take him to his potty spot and don't allow him to play on these outings or your dog may begin ringing the bell to get out when he doesn't need to relieve himself.

Photo Courtesy of Lucy Bowe

Using the Crate for Potty Training

The crate is a great tool to use for potty training because it allows you to control your puppy in a small space during the times you can't supervise him. If you're using a wire crate, make sure the area is big enough for your dog to comfortably stand and turn around in but not big enough that he can take several steps from side to side. This will prevent him from soiling one side and sleeping on the other.

If you're not sure how often you should take your dog outside, a good rule of thumb to follow for a young puppy is for every month old he is, that's how many hours he can wait to go potty. That doesn't mean that you should only take your puppy out that often, because if you do, you will most likely be cleaning up a lot of accidents. This is simply a general guideline for how long a young puppy can be left in the crate before needing to go out. Never leave your puppy or dog in the crate longer than four to six hours except at night, when you should only take him out as he wakes.

When you get up in the morning, immediately take your dog outside to the designated potty area. If you're planning to put your dog back into the crate while you're gone for work, take the time to exercise him thoroughly before you do. This will help your dog rest better while you're gone. You will need to come home to let your dog out at lunchtime. Follow the same procedure before putting him back into the crate.

If you can't get back home to take your dog out at lunch, you will need to make other arrangements. Doggy daycare is a great option. It will help you continue the potty-training process and also help with socialization. Usually, those places require certain vaccinations, so be sure to call and check ahead of time. If doggy daycare is not an option, call a friend or family member to come by and let your puppy out for you. You can even hire a dog walker to come and exercise your pup while you are away. Go through a reputable service like Care.com so you can read references and know they've had a background check.

If you absolutely have to leave your dog in the crate or a puppy-proofed room for longer than you should, you can use a puppy pad on one side of the crate. This will slow down the training process because you will, at some point, have to remove the pads and retrain your dog that the only acceptable place to go is outside. Remember, Whoodles are not happy alone and may become anxious. If you are planning to leave your dog home every day while you are at work, you should reconsider owning one.

The First Few Weeks

The first few weeks of potty training your Whoodle will be challenging. In the beginning, take your dog out every hour or so during daytime hours. He may not need to go every time but give him 10 to 15 minutes to try. Even if you have a fenced backyard, it will benefit you to take your dog outside on a leash. This will allow you to control where he goes and help him not be too distracted. Don't forget to praise him verbally and with a treat as soon as he finishes. This is an important step in helping him realize this is what you want him to do.

Photo Courtesy of Brent Boyle

How to Handle Accidents

Accidents are going to happen, so go ahead and buy that odor-neutralizing cleaner! Learning to potty outside is tough for a young puppy and requires patience by all. If you have been trying to train your dog to go on the grass, accidents on rugs and carpets are inevitable. The feeling of the carpet on a dog's paws is very similar to the feeling of grass and can sometimes trick a young puppy into thinking he can relieve himself there. If this becomes a problem, you might want to temporarily remove any rugs from your puppy's designated area until he gets the hang of going outside.

If you catch your dog in the act, quickly pick him up and take him outside to the potty area. Don't punish or yell at your dog. Most often, accidents are a direct result of the owner not taking the dog out enough. Sometimes a dog will soil a carpet just minutes after coming inside. Regardless, your puppy is still learning and should not be punished for the mistake. Punishing will only confuse your dog and prolong the potty-training process.

If your dog does pee or poop inside, never clean up the accident in front of him. Dogs typically return to the same spot repeatedly, so you have to clean it thoroughly with an odor neutralizer made specifically for pet urine. This will help remove the smell that keeps the dog coming back.

Stories from a Whoodle Owner

Willow

Housebreaking Triumphs

Like most other dogs, when Willow was being housebroken, she made no connection between peeing and pooping – they were completely different and unrelated functions. She understood right away that it was not okay to poop indoors and ever since she was a little puppy has never made a mistake inside. But getting her to pee outside took more time and effort. A great technique was making a really big deal every time she peed on her wee-wee pad and, later, outside with hand-clapping and cheers to make her feel really special, as well as giving her a treat. Another creative trick was to say the word "wee-wee" (you can choose your own word as long as it's consistent) every time she squatted down. As a result, Willow pees on command whenever I use the word. It's very convenient.

If you are having issues with your dog urinating in the house, you can purchase a black light that reveals any spots of urine you may have missed. These lights are very affordable and can save you a major headache cleaning up messes you didn't know your dog was making!

Pros and Cons of Doggy Doors

Doggy doors can be beneficial in your efforts to potty train, especially for older dogs. If you have a secured backyard, a doggy door can allow your dog to let himself out as he pleases. This could mean fewer accidents and a shorter training period. You should never let your dog go outside unsupervised unless you know the backyard is completely secure and your dog can't escape. Adding a doggy door is not for everyone, though, and you should review this list of pros and cons before making your decision.

INSTALLATION: Installing a doggy door is making a permanent change to your home, and they are notoriously difficult to install. If you don't own your home, a doggy door is probably not an option for you.

UNWANTED VISITORS: Doggy doors are great for allowing your dog to freely come in and out of your home, but they may unintentionally offer that same freedom to unwanted wild animals as well. Nobody wants a tiny masked bandit coming in under the cover of night! However, this could be solved by getting a doggy door that stays locked until it senses a microchip in your dog's collar as he approaches.

INDOOR CATS: If you have an indoor cat, it will be nearly impossible to keep him from leaving through an unlocked doggy door. If your cat has been declawed, this is particularly dangerous because your cat will have no defense from predators. If you have an indoor cat who already loves to go outside, a doggy door will allow him to bring his "treasures" inside the house. Finding a dead snake or bird in the house is probably not what you want.

SECURING THE YARD: Before allowing your dog unsupervised time in the yard, you must be sure it's a safe area. Be sure the fence is secure and add a lock to any gate so neighborhood kids or thieves cannot let your dog out. If your Whoodle is a digger, then you may have a problem with him burrowing out to go explore. This is dangerous because he may encounter cars on his big adventure outside the yard.

BACKYARD POOL: Another danger to consider in the backyard is a pool. Even if your dog enjoys swimming, he should never be allowed near the pool unless you are out there with him. Swimming alone is dangerous, even for a dog. Allowing full access to the house and pool also permits your dog to come in and out freely while sopping wet, causing a big mess for you to clean up when you get home.

FIRE ESCAPE: One positive to a doggy door is it allows your dog to escape the house in case of an emergency. This could potentially save your dog's life in the event of a fire.

If you know your yard is safe and secure and you want to install a doggy door to aid in training, go ahead! You will still need to confine your dog's indoor privileges to a small space while allowing access to the doggy door. This can be done by using a playpen set up against the wall.

A doggy door is not always a good option, but in the right scenario, it can be very helpful. For elderly or disabled owners who have a more difficult time getting around, a doggy door allows the dog to relieve himself in the proper area without any burden to the owner.

If you decide on a doggy door, be prepared for some training. The first time you teach your Whoodle to use it, give him a gentle push through and have another person on the other side, ready with a small treat and plenty of praise. Do this several times, in both directions.

Once your puppy allows you to push him through without resistance, go to the opposite side of the doggy door, extend your hand through to the puppy, and allow him to smell the treat in your hand. Use the treat to lure him through. Finally, call him from the other side, and give a treat when he goes through by himself. If you spend 5 or 10 minutes a day doing this, your Whoodle should be going through the door by himself within a week.

CHAPTER 7

Socializing Your Whoodle

Importance of Socialization

Whoodles are generally friendly to all, adults and kids alike. Though they are part Terrier, they are easy-going and typically greet other people and dogs with a friendly tail wag. However, like any other dog, they need regular and early socialization.

Photo Courtesy of Amanda Jaggers

By beginning your dog's socialization early, you can be sure that he will be able to coexist with any people or dogs he encounters in any environment. This will make life easier for you if you take your dog to the park, restaurants or other crowded outdoor events.

Behavior Around Other Dogs

Imagine a world where people greeted each other the way dogs do by sniffing, circling and jumping up and down playfully. Luckily for us, we humans have strict social guidelines to follow when we encounter each other. Dogs also have a set of social rules, but they are a bit different from ours.

Much like people, dogs greet each other differently at a first meeting than they greet an old friend and much of it depends on the individual dog's personality. Dogs typically greet each other in one or all of the following ways:

SNIFFING: Probably the most notable canine ritual is the sniff test. When dogs greet one another, they may begin with the muzzle or go straight for the backside. Sometimes the sniff will be brief and sometimes it can seem like a full-blown investigation. Unless one dog seems uncomfortable, this is perfectly normal behavior and doesn't need to be stopped. Once the dogs have satisfied their sniffers, they can move on to the next step in the canine greeting.

PLAY STANCE: Have you ever seen a dog approach another dog and immediately go into a play bow? This behavior is simply one dog attempting to initiate play with another. It's like he's saying, "Hey there! Do you want to be friends and play together?" Even a quick, playful growl accompanied by a friendly tail wag is acceptable. Again, as long as neither dog seems stressed, there is no need to stop this behavior.

HELPFUL TIP
More Than Just the Dog Park

Whoodles have a reputation for being friendly and well-tempered dogs, but their high energy level makes it particularly important to practice good socialization at an early age. While socializing your dog with other dogs and people is an important part of this training, there is another important element. In addition to human and canine socialization, try to introduce your puppy to a variety of sounds during the first 16 weeks of life, including ringtones, the vacuum cleaner, and other household appliances, as well as a variety of different surfaces, such as grass and tile. Early exposure to these experiences can minimize your dog's stress in future social settings.

Even if the other dog declines the offer to play, that doesn't mean the meeting was not successful.

EXERTING DOMINANCE: This particular greeting is probably the least endearing but is still acceptable in the canine world. One dog may exert his dominance by being the first to sniff and by non-aggressively showing the other dog he is in charge. This could include mounting. This process may be obvious to you, or it may all happen so quickly that you don't even notice until little Sparky rolls over to show his belly in submission.

As with the other behaviors, these are the natural social ways of dogs and should not be -stopped unless there is real aggression or stress. Dogs take social cues well and are pretty good at keeping each other in line. If one dog is displeased, he will probably let the other know quickly.

Safe Ways to Socialize with Other Pets

The way dogs behave around each other can vary from breed to breed and dog to dog. If you're bringing your Whoodle home as a puppy, socializing him with other dogs should be easy. In general, puppies are more adaptable and willing to meet other dogs.

Socialization should begin as early as possible but be sure not to allow your puppy to have close contact with dogs you don't know until he has had his complete series of puppy shots. This may mean only socializing with other close family pets until your Whoodle is a little older.

Depending on where you live, socializing your Whoodle may be easier or more challenging. If you live in the city with your Whoodle in an apartment or a highly populated area, you will probably encounter many dogs on your walks outside. This provides a great opportunity to meet and interact with dogs on a regular basis. Be aware of other dogs and their owners, however. If the walker is walking multiple dogs at once or isn't paying attention, do not let your Whoodle approach them.

Although you will encounter more dogs in the more densely populated areas, you will need to wait until your Whoodle puppy is older before you take him out at all to avoid coming into contact with harmful viruses.

On the other hand, if you live in a more rural area, your dog may have more off-leash freedoms but less opportunity to organically interact with other dogs on a regular basis. If this is the case for your Whoodle, make sure you are intentional with socialization early on before bad habits are formed.

Stories from a Whoodle Owner

Flynn

Best Friends Forever

As soon as your new puppy has completed their vaccinations (typically at about 12 weeks of age), they are ready to start the all-important socialization process. Our friends, with their Golden Retriever Nuka, were eager to meet him, and Nuka was already providing socialization for a Golden Doodle puppy a few months older than Flynn. Perfect! So off we went for Flynn's first meeting with dogs outside of his mom and littermates. We all gathered in the little fenced in back yard, and Nuka promptly told the new puppy where his place was in the hierarchy (at the very bottom, of course). Izzie, the Doodle puppy, took one look at Flynn and declared that he was her new best friend, and she was going to teach him how to play. We could barely restrain ourselves; the mayhem looked so scary! Flynn would raise his tail and wag it, and bounce a few inches, and Izzie would pounce on him. Flynn would flee back to someone's lap, and regroup. In a few seconds, he would try again, and over the course of the next half hour, he and Izzie were soon tussling happily...until his sharp little puppy teeth connected with her tender ear, or lip, or whatever he tried to latch onto. She would yelp and shake him off, and put her much larger mouth on him.

Like all puppies given appropriate socialization, Flynn learned quickly to moderate his bite (it's called bite control). He also learned how to signal that he wants to play, or to say, "enough, back off please". Over the next few months, he and Izzie and Nuka had play dates at least once a week, and usually more. By the end of that first year, Izzie and Flynn were best buddies, and they have stayed tight friends since. They go to the groomer together for company and mutual comfort, and still have weekly play dates. Seeing them greet each other, bounding forward and frolicking wildly, is pure joy.

On-Leash Socialization

There are two main methods for introducing your dog to another: on-leash or off-leash. If you choose to socialize your puppy with a leash on, keep your puppy close on a leash or on the other side of a barrier, such as a gate when you make introductions with other dogs, especially those that are older or larger. Preferably, all other dogs should also be leashed or somehow restrained in case anything goes wrong.

Allow the dogs to greet each other for a few seconds, then walk away. Each owner should distract his dog at this point until they are no longer interested in the other dog. If the initial interaction went well, allow the dogs to come together again in the same manner. Keep the leash loose so the dog can maneuver but not so loose it becomes a tangled mess.

Read each dog's body language to determine how the greeting is going. Bodies should be relaxed, and there should be no staring contests. As the dogs become comfortable and relaxed with each other, you will be able to let them off-leash, so they can have supervised play.

Off- Leash Socialization

Some trainers believe first-time dog greetings should always be done off-leash so that the dogs behave and greet each other more naturally. They believe that some dogs will feel trapped by the leash and become more defensive in nature, making the greeting unnatural and awkward. If this is the method you choose, make sure the owners of both dogs are fully compliant and willing to meet in a safe and neutral fenced area.

A first-time greeting should never be done in one of the dogs' yards. This could be seen as an invasion of territory for some dogs and cause a defensive reaction. Allow the dogs to meet but monitor their body language. If they use the body language described above, you don't need to interfere. But if either dog seems stiff, uncomfortable or agitated, separate the dogs and use distractions to get their attention off of each other.

Off-leash greetings can bring a greater risk if you don't know the other dog well and should only be done with friendly, pre-socialized dogs. Safety is the most important thing when socializing your dog, so only do what makes you feel comfortable.

Socializing Adult Dogs

If you're bringing an adult Whoodle into your home, the socialization process may take some extra time and careful planning. Depending on the dog's previous situation, he may not be used to other dogs. Often with a rescue, you don't know exactly what his life has held up until this point. He may have been kept in a cage his whole life, abused by his owner, or even previously attacked by a dog. All of these things are unknowns that could have a significant impact on his social abilities.

Be patient with your dog, no matter his age, and allow him to socialize on his terms. If your dog seems to have trouble socializing, take it slow and

Photo Courtesy of Ariel Jamil

avoid putting your dog in situations that will cause him stress. This will only cause setbacks.

When dealing with an unsocialized adult dog, begin slowly at home. Take your dog on a walk around your neighborhood where he can see other dogs indirectly. He should eventually become comfortable enough to walk by other dogs in their backyards or on leashes without becoming stressed. When he has successfully mastered these indirect encounters, it's time to move on to the next step.

If you have a neighbor with a dog, this is a great place to start direct socialization. These dogs will probably encounter each other at one point or another and will benefit by getting to know each other. Ask your neighbor to arrange a time to allow both dogs to meet, on leashes, in a neutral part of the yard.

Take things slow and give them space if either seems stressed. Follow the three-second rule then walk away and distract each dog. Allow the dogs to come together again if the first encounter went well. If it doesn't seem to be going well, that's okay! Allow the dogs to just be in the yard at the same time until they become used to each other, then gradually allow them to interact more as it seems appropriate.

Keep your demeanor calm and stress-free so that your dog doesn't pick up on any tension. It's all about establishing trust between you and your dog and between your dog and your neighbor's dog. Speak to your neighbor and his dog in a friendly and confident tone to help show your Whoodle that the visitors are not a threat. With enough positive interactions, your dog should eventually warm up to them and become more social.

If you don't have a neighboring dog, call a friend with a dog or take your dog to a dog park or run. A dog park can be overwhelming, depending on how many dogs are there and whether their owners are adequately supervising them. This may be a last resort as a place to socialize.

Begin by just walking around the perimeter at a comfortable distance. Listen to your dog and take his cues. If he seems comfortable, allow him to interact more closely with a dog through the fence. If he remains calm, praise him.

Reward him for positive encounters and remove him from negative ones. Try to only let him interact with dogs that are also calm. It will not help the situation to engage with a loud, barking, rambunctious dog through the fence. This could cause stress for an unsocialized dog and stop progress.

Another great option for socializing your Whoodle with other dogs is to enroll him in a daytime care facility or in beginner obedience classes at a local training center. Call your local pet supply store or ask your breeder for referrals. This should only be done after he has had his full series of puppy shots and is beginning to mature.

For obedience classes, arrive at least 10 to 15 minutes before the class begins and sit quietly with your dog (on his lead) so that he can get accustomed to the environment and begin to feel confident with other dogs.

Once the class begins, he will be focused on learning some basics of obedience, while surrounded by other dogs. You will also learn how to teach your Whoodle valuable commands, like heel, sit, stay and come, which will come in very handy throughout his life.

Photo Courtesy of Julie Stajduhar

Greeting New People

Introducing a Whoodle puppy to new people should be easy. Puppies are generally easygoing and take to new friends well, especially with the friendly nature of the Whoodle.

If you live in a densely populated area and you are quarantining your dog at home for the first seven weeks as discussed earlier, you will still need to socialize your Whoodle pup with as many people as possible during this time. Invite people over and try to introduce your Whoodle to 100 people within those first seven weeks. Make sure you have your guests remove their shoes before entering so they do not track in anything harmful. This rule applies to Whoodles in a rural area as well.

Photo Courtesy of Rayna and Michael Grenon

One challenge common for Whoodles is jumping. While a small, fluffy, jumping Whoodle may seem cute to some, to many it is a source of irritation. It's much harder to correct the behavior if it was once allowed. With their naturally energetic disposition, Whoodles can easily form bad jumping habits that are difficult to break.

Ideally, when approached by a person, your pup should remain calm and keep all four paws on the ground. To stop a jumping habit, begin by teaching your dog an alternate command. "Sit" is a good command to combat jumping because your dog can't do both at the same time. (Learn more about teaching basic commands in Chapter 10.)

When your dog gets overly excited and begins to jump, counter by giving the "sit" command. Reward him for sitting and staying still. If he can't stay calm and continues to jump, leave the room and ignore your dog for 30 seconds. Return and try again. This process works well for meeting new people, getting the leash out for walks, or any other exciting event that gets your dog jumping. And for a Whoodle, lots of things are jump worthy!

Stories from a Whoodle Owner

Willow

The Queen of the Dog Park

Willow is the belle of the dog run. She is on the meet-and-greet committee, saying hello to every dog and dog owner who enters. Her favorite playmates are other doodles. She loves to chase them and be chased, trying every trick in the book to get them to give her a run for her money. She has no clue how to fetch. She just loves to grab a ball or stick and prance around with it.

But her most endearing behavior in the dog run is what I call the "Willow treatment." She has her favorite group of humans who hang out on one of the benches every morning, drinking their coffee. When I let her loose in the run, she can barely contain her joy at seeing them. She tears across the gravel to greet them, joining them on the bench and showering each person with enthusiastic face licks, usually with her front paws on their chest so they can't resist. When she's done, she jumps off the bench to repeat her ritual with each of their dogs, a group of seniors who pretend they are annoyed but secretly welcome her antics.

Introducing a Rescue Whoodle

Introducing a rescue dog to new people can be a different story. Not knowing your dog's past means not knowing if he's had any negative human interactions. Begin any new introductions with people much like you would with dogs, slow and controlled. If your rescue Whoodle is socially stunted, you'll have to work to gain his trust. Apply those same principles to anyone you want to introduce to your dog.

If you're having guests over, ask those people ahead of time to remain calm and not show the dog much attention. This may help ease your dog's mind and keep him settled. If your guests want to rub and love all over your Whoodle, even with good intentions, it could cause him to become overexcited and stressed.

Once calm and comfortable, your dog may be trusting enough to allow a belly rub or two, but it should always be on his terms. Give your guests some training treats to gain his trust. If your dog is particularly shy and nervous, and you don't see much progress being made, try separating him with a baby gate so that he can observe the people but not feel pressured or overwhelmed.

If your Whoodle is having trouble becoming comfortable with people, don't be afraid to take your dog to your local big-box home improvement store. Most of these stores not only allow dogs, but welcome them warmly. It can be a great place to get him comfortable with people at a distance.

It's hard to make your way from the electrical department to the lumber area without a dozen or so friendly people asking to say hello and pet your adorable Whoodle. No doubt people will be dying to know what this adorable, fluffy-faced dog is. Have a few small treats handy and ask people to give one to your puppy. He will quickly learn that meeting people is a good experience.

Whoodles and Children

Whoodles and children get along very well and can develop wonderful relationships. Due to the Whoodle's moderate size, he can fit in well with an active child's lifestyle. His energetic, playful nature will make him the perfect playmate and companion.

While it may be cute to allow your Whoodle puppy to sleep with your children, never allow it. Depending on the size and age of your Whoodle, he may be relatively small. Accidentally rolling over on top of your puppy while sleeping is dangerous and could even be fatal.

Teach your children to be gentle and kind, never pulling ears, hair or a tail. Show them by example the proper way to pet and handle your Whoodle so that they understand how to safely handle him. No matter how friendly and trustworthy your dog is, never leave a child and dog alone unattended. This is for the safety of both the child and the dog.

Interspecies Introductions

The Whoodle possesses a higher than average prey drive and it will make him more apt to chase small animals and other objects. Keep smaller animals, such as birds, rodents, and rabbits, away from your Whoodle if they don't need to interact. If you have a pet of another species that you want to meet with your Whoodle, begin the introductions as young as possible and with constant supervision. You may not ever be able to fully trust a Whoodle with small animals.

Introducing Your Whoodle to a Cat

To introduce your new Whoodle puppy to a resident cat, begin by keeping the animals separated and place a blanket or toy with the puppy's scent near the cat. Do the same for the puppy in a different area of the house. Let the dog and the cat sniff and become accustomed to the scents before a face-to-face interaction. Keep in mind, your Whoodle's prey drive may cause him to want to chase your cat, so you need to introduce them as young as possible to avoid this bad habit before it begins.

After exchanging scents, allow your pets to interact indirectly. Keep them separated by a gate or the crate but allow them to view each other. Depending on their reactions, you may feel comfortable enough to let them loose, but be careful. Your puppy probably can't do much damage to your cat at his young age, but your cat can definitely harm your puppy if he feels threatened. Try introductions with someone gently holding each animal. Let the two sniff and explore but watch carefully for claws. Praise both animals for calm and reasonable reactions. Stop the introduction immediately if there is any fear or aggression shown.

Most likely, your Whoodle pup will want to make friends with your cat and play, or chase, right away. Your cat, on the other hand, may not know how to handle all of this playful affection and will need a place to escape. This escape should be off the ground in an area where your dog can't reach. Always allow your cat to have access to his safe place.

Stories from a Whoodle Owner

Flynn the Whoodle and Tigger the Barn Cat

Flynn got to meet our barn cat, Tigger, within a day or two of coming home with us. Tigger was raised with dogs, so he was happy that we had brought one home for him. He licked Flynn, grooming him like he was a kitten, and Flynn licked him in return. Their bonding continued to grow as Flynn grew, and by the time Flynn was a few months old, they were having adventures together.

Flynn was a January puppy and winter lasts well into the spring here in Vermont. By late May, he and Tigger were good buddies and Tigger was teaching Flynn how to be a barn cat. Flynn learned how to sit on the back stoop with Tigger after dark, with the light shining through the window in the door, hunting June bugs. These fat, slow-flying beetles would hit the glass window, seeking the light, and Tigger would jump up and knock them down. The dazed bugs crawled around re-orienting themselves, but before they could take off, Tigger showed Flynn how to pounce on them and gobble them down. Oh yum, what a great high-protein snack! They would sit there companionably for half an hour at a stretch, catching June bugs and feeding them to each other.

Tigger is a great barn cat; he's a terrific hunter and keeps the rodent population in our llama barn and garden down to a dull roar. He took his responsibilities for raising Flynn seriously, and developed a full curriculum to teach him what he would need to know. Tigger brought Flynn "presents" every day; we learned to watch where we stepped when we walked out the door, avoiding the dead mice littering the doorstep. Flynn was appreciative of these presents, but with our help, he quickly learned to simply nose them in grateful acknowledgment, then leave them for Tigger to consume.

Introducing an Older Whoodle

You will need to take a different approach to introducing an adult Whoodle to a resident cat. An adult Whoodle can potentially chase and seriously harm your cat while your cat can also cause your dog significant harm. Begin with the scent exchange described above.

After a day of getting accustomed to the other's scent, allow the two animals to meet through a closed door. Depending on personality, they may not be interested or they may be busting down the door to see who is on the other side. Allow each animal to become calm and relaxed before any face-to-face interactions.

Once the two have become relaxed and calm on both sides of the door, allow the animals to meet with the dog on a loose leash. The leash is a safety precaution for your cat, so don't skip that step. Allow a brief interaction before separating them and diverting their attention. If the initial interaction was calm and peaceful, praise them both and try again.

If you decide to let the two interact with your dog off-leash, always ensure your cat can escape to his safe space, designated just for him. Cats and dogs can coexist peacefully together and form close bonds, but it probably won't happen overnight for your cat or Whoodle. Give it time and patience and you will see the benefits of your effort.

Aggression and Bad Behavior

Whoodles don't typically have issues with aggression unless they have been traumatized or allowed to behave poorly. Animal abuse can cause deep-seated issues for your dog, which can manifest as growling, snapping or biting at you or other pets. This is especially important to remember if you're bringing home an adult rescue dog with an unknown past.

If your dog displays aggressive behaviors, the first thing you need to do is take your dog to the vet to be sure there is no underlying condition causing him pain. Occasionally, a grumpy dog can be the result of invisible pain you didn't know he was dealing with.

Once injury or any other underlying condition is ruled out, it's time to evaluate the dog's current situation. Is there anything causing your Whoodle unnecessary stress? Is he being left alone too long? Is he being given enough attention and exercise? A Whoodle demands a high level of activity and companionship, so his behavior could suffer from not getting it. Much like a child, he could be acting out to get your attention.

If your Whoodle is showing aggression toward other dogs, take the proper steps to socialize him. Go slowly and don't progress to direct interactions until your dog can keep calm consistently. For dogs dealing with aggression issues, this could take much longer to achieve and you should be very careful.

If your dog is showing aggression toward other pets at home, begin by identifying the source. Is it food aggression? Does your dog become possessive over toys or treats? If you identify the source, remove it.

Feed your Whoodle in another room, away from all other pets and remove toys he is possessive over. Only allow him to have the toy in the confines of his crate or designated alone area. Removing your dog from the stressful situation will not solve the aggression problem, but it will make life easier while you deal with the root cause.

As long as your dog isn't causing any physical harm to you or any other members of your family, continue to work on carefully socializing the dog, rewarding friendly behavior with treats and praise. If the aggression doesn't improve or evolves to physical harm in any way, seek a professional trainer's help immediately. Never leave a potentially aggressive dog alone with another animal or an unfamiliar person.

What to Do When Pets Don't Get Along

If your Whoodle and other pets cannot seem to get along after using these tips to ease the transition, don't hesitate to call a professional trainer. The sooner you address the issue, the easier it will be to overcome. Allowing your pets to continue coexisting in a stress-filled environment can amplify the problem and could even lead to injury. Sometimes a trained professional is able to address issues you were unable to recognize yourself.

How to Break up a Fight

If worse comes to worst and you find yourself in a situation needing to break up a dog fight, it is important you know how to do so safely. The best way to separate two fighting dogs is by using the wheelbarrow method. This is where you grab each dog by the back legs and pull them away from each other. In order to safely use this method, you need one person restraining each dog this way.

If you are alone and need to separate two dogs, distract the dogs with a loud noise long enough to separate the two so they cannot continue the aggression. Water also works well to divert their attention if there is a water hose nearby. You can also find a barrier to physically separate the dogs. This could be a chair, a board or anything else you have on hand.

Never try to get between two fighting dogs with your body or hands. This could lead to injury, putting you and the dogs in more danger.

Is It Really Aggression or Just Rough Play?

Many dogs growl and bare their teeth when they play. This does not mean your dog has aggression issues. In fact, sometimes, it can be quite difficult to distinguish between play and aggression.

When your dog and another dog are playfully bowing and taking turns chasing, rolling over and mouthing each other, these are all signs that they are engaging in play together. Allowing this play to continue offers your dog great practice with social skills and is a wonderful outlet for the excess energy of a healthy Whoodle pup.

If the dogs are playing, but one or both seem stiff and tense, there may be more than a playful romp going on between them. Deep, drawn-out growling, staring into the other dog's eyes and a one-sided chase may all be indications that one or both of the dogs are showing some real aggression. You may need to end the encounter quickly before things escalate.

If you're having trouble with your puppy or adult dog playing too rough with you, the best thing to do is ignore him. In a pack of dogs, older dogs will naturally teach the younger pups when enough is enough. They do this by verbal cues then ending play immediately. Even puppies of the same litter do this to each other.

As the owner, you can take the same stance. When play becomes too rough, give a loud verbal "yip" and walk away, ignoring your dog. After a minute, once the dog seems to have shifted his attention, return to play. Repeat this process until the puppy understands the rough play is not acceptable. Eventually, he will understand and will lessen his intensity. This is a natural learning process for your dog and he should not be punished in the process.

Also be aware of how you approach your dog for play. If you come in swinging your hands and arms around, this is encouraging your dog to play rough. Use toys instead of your body and keep movements gentle to prevent play from getting too rowdy.

CHAPTER 8

Exercising Your Whoodle – Physically and Mentally

Exercise Requirements

Photo Courtesy of Alyssa Harding

Being a high-energy breed, your Whoodle will need ample exercise to keep him happy and healthy. Shoot for a minimum of a mile-long, brisk walk every day. If this seems daunting, break it up into multiple, shorter walks throughout the day.

If caring for the physical requirements of a Whoodle seems too much for you, consider a different breed as Whoodles will suffer greatly without sufficient exercise. If you live in apartments, lead a sedentary life or spend most of the day away from home, a Whoodle may not be suitable for your lifestyle. You might consider a mini-Whoodle instead, as they will need slightly less exercise than their standard-sized counterparts.

City Dogs Versus Rural Dogs

For Whoodles living in a densely populated area such as a city, dog runs, day-care and other indoor exercise options may be good solutions when there is limited space for exercising outdoors. For dogs residing in a more rural area, hiking, trail running and swimming may be suitable.

Stories from a Whoodle Owner

Willow

FRAP – Frenetic Random Activity Period

Be prepared for the late night puppy crazies. There's even a name for it: Frenetic Random Activity Period (FRAP), also known as the Zoomies. Don't be alarmed – this is completely normal and your Whoodle will outgrow this behavior when he gets older. For now, you can just sit back and enjoy the show.

As a puppy, Willow was definitely a Frapper (aka Baby Zoomer). When she returned from her evening walk, she would grab a toy, shoe or slipper, and go wild, racing madly around the couches in the living room at full speed, jumping on and off furniture, stopping on a dime, changing directions, skidding across floors and ignoring all commands to come or sit. Then, her zoomie would end as suddenly as it began and the exhausted puppy would flop down and promptly fall asleep.

Options for Exercising Your Whoodle

Walking or running the block a few times is a great way to fit exercise into your Whoodle's routine if you are able, but it can be a challenge for some and become a little mundane for both of you over time. Add in some unique activities to spice things up so both you and your Whoodle enjoy this crucial time together. Changing things up occasionally will also keep him mentally engaged. With both indoor and outdoor options, there is sure to be an activity perfect for you and your Whoodle on the following list!

FLIRT POLE –A Flirt Pole allows you to engage your dog in a game of chase without much movement of your own. This device is basically a stick with a toy attached to the end by a string. If you are disabled or have limited mobility, you can even use the flirt pole from a seated position. The flirt pole engages your dog mentally and physically; it's a win-win!

Photo Courtesy of Kate Kennedy

PLAY HIDE AND SEEK – Once your dog has mastered basic commands (more on basic commands in Chapter 10) and can sit and stay, try engaging him in a game of hide and seek. Take your dog to a designated location in the house and have him sit and stay where he is. Your job is to go hide somewhere else in the house then call him when you are ready.

If your dog won't stay still long enough to allow you to hide, try giving him a treat that will take him half a minute or so to finish. Once he finishes, call to him from your hiding place and see how long it takes him to find you. Keep giving your Whoodle verbal encouragement until he discovers you. This is a great way to exercise your dog on a rainy or cold day.

> **HELPFUL TIP**
> **Dog Puzzles**
>
> Whoodles love to be entertained and mentally stimulated, so if you plan to leave your dog alone for a few hours, you'll need to provide plenty of boredom busters so your Whoodle doesn't decide to entertain himself with your favorite pair of slippers. Dog puzzles are a great way to keep your Whoodle's mind busy. Most of these puzzles revolve around hiding a treat or squeaker inside a complicated mechanism that your dog will have to figure out

PLAY FETCH – Is there a dog in the world that doesn't love a good game of fetch? If there is, he's probably not a Whoodle! This classic game can be played with a tennis ball, rope or Frisbee. Mix it up to keep things interesting. Teach your dog to return the item to your lap and this game can be a consistently easy outlet for excess energy, especially if your Whoodle is still hyped up after his daily walk.

Fetch can be played on a larger scale outdoors or inside a house or an apartment. This activity can work for anyone!

SCAVENGER HUNT – Did you know a typical dog has up to 300 million olfactory receptors in his nose and the part of a dog's brain devoted to smell is proportionally 40 times larger than a human's? Simply put, that means your Whoodle has a powerful sniffer. This game will make mealtime or snack time fun by putting that nose to work.

Hide small amounts of food or treats around a room and see if your dog can sniff them out. If you hide them in enough areas, he may find himself running around the room from spot to spot trying to find the source of the smell. While this may not provide as much exercise as one of the previous suggestions, it is still a way to give your Whoodle some form of exercise without leaving the house. Just make sure you remember where you hid the food so it isn't left there when the game is over.

DOG RUNS – Dog runs are especially helpful for those who have limited access to green space. Take advantage of the open area within a fence to

Photo Courtesy of Diane Crowley

allow your dog to run free in a safe way. This also allows you to sit while your dog gets his energy out. Be sure to follow all park rules for safe and fun play for all.

PLAY DATES – Play dates are great for any Whoodle, but especially helpful for those dogs who need more socialization. Seek out other dog owners, family or friends, and coordinate a time to regularly get your dogs together to play. You may take turns hosting this play date at each other's home or you may plan to meet up at a public dog park.

A good way for your Whoodle to meet dogs to play with is by introducing yourself to other dog owners you encounter while you are out. This may be on a walk or it may be an owner you meet on a trip to the dog run. Be sure to only plan play dates with people and dogs you trust.

DOG DAY CARE – Even if you spend most of your time home with your Whoodle, an occasional trip to a local doggy day care is a great way to give your pup some play time with other dogs. This will provide him with important socialization opportunities and mental stimulation. After a few hours at day care, your Whoodle will probably be ready for a relaxing nap at home.

AGILITY TRAINING – Though Whoodles are not known for agility, learning any new skill with your dog, especially one that requires much physical exercise, is a great way for both of you to stay fit and healthy while strengthening your trust and bond. Who knows, your Whoodle may be the next agility champion in training!

Flyball is another different, competitive game dogs of all breeds can compete in. In this sport, a team of four dogs complete a relay race over hurdles to retrieve tennis balls from a box.

In order to retrieve the ball, each dog must jump on a spring-loaded box which releases the ball. Much like agility, your Whoodle must learn to maneuver obstacles to complete the task set before him. Both flyball and agility competitions are a great way to exercise an energetic dog and meet fellow dog owners.

HIRE A SERVICE – If you are unable to care for your Whoodle's exercise needs on your own, you can hire a dog walker through websites such as Care.com or Rover.com. Some locally based companies such as HikeDoggie.com, based in Colorado, even offer to take your dog out for a hike for you a minimum of once a week.

If you decide to hire a service to exercise your dog, make sure you only hire someone you trust to care for your Whoodle.

Exercise Needs by Age

Your Whoodle's exercise needs will evolve and change as he ages. While all of the exercise options mentioned above are suitable for a healthy adult Whoodle, they may not all be suitable for a young Whoodle pup or an aging senior dog.

Photo Courtesy of Erin Hastings

EXERCISING A WHOODLE PUPPY: While you may think your energetic young pup can handle anything, be aware that there are risks of overexerting his growing body. Young pups, before the age of 12 to 18 months are at an elevated risk of growth-plate injuries.

Growth plates are the soft regions at the end of your dog's bones. These growth plates harden as your dog matures, but remain vulnerable to injury until then. Severe injury to the growth plates in the first year of life can result in deformities that may require surgery. Signs of growth plate injury include swelling, limping, stiffness and pain.

While growth plate injuries can occur from basic activities, such as climbing stairs and jumping on and off furniture, they are more likely to result from strenuous exercises such as hiking, climbing and even running.

To prevent injury, keep your pup happy and healthy by exercising him in a safe way. Keep strenuous activity to a minimum and focus on short walks and some of the less intense activities mentioned above, such as hide and seek, fetch or scavenger hunts.

If you hire someone to exercise your Whoodle pup, make sure they are knowledgeable about what is developmentally appropriate for his age and stage of life. The same rules apply for doggy day care centers. Young puppies should not be left to play with adult dogs as they may injure themselves trying to keep up.

EXERCISING A SENIOR WHOODLE: Just as with Whoodle puppies, senior dogs need extra care and attention to prevent serious injury. Even as an older dog slows down and requires less intense exercise, it is still important to keep him moving in a safe way.

Slow-paced walks and shorter play times will satisfy your senior Whoodle's needs without overexerting him. If your dog begins to limp or seems to be in pain, see a veterinarian to check for arthritis. He or she can prescribe a treatment plan to ease his pain. Arthritis is common in older dogs and can be successfully managed with the right care plan.

A great low-impact exercise for older dogs, especially those with arthritis, is swimming. This activity can keep your dog heart healthy without exerting pressure on his joints.

Importance of Mental Exercise

Although physical exercise usually gets most of the attention, mental stimulation for your Whoodle is equally as important. A bored dog is often a destructive dog, especially with a high-energy and high-intelligence dog like the Whoodle.

Stories from a Whoodle Owner

Willow

Mental Exercise

Whoodles are high-energy dogs that require a lot of mental and physical exercise. In addition to playing, running, swimming and digging, Willow likes to be amused even when she is not in motion. She will happily work on a bone for minutes at a time. She loves the outdoors and will sit on the sidewalk in the city or on the deck upstate for hours, contentedly watching, smelling, and listening to the goings-on, mostly things I myself am unable to detect.

Our third floor corner apartment in the city has lovely views of the street below. Willow loves looking out of the windows but, unfortunately for her, we have radiator covers that are built out around 12 inches from the windows, which prevent her from getting a good look at what's going on. So, we got her a doggie staircase. It took her some time to master, but once she got the hang of it, she climbs up and sits or lies on the radiator cover and happily watches the world go by. I think she thinks she's a cat.

Tips for Keeping Your Whoodle Occupied

Many of the exercise suggestions mentioned above serve as both mental exercise and physical. Playing hide and seek, doing scavenger hunts and using a flirt pole all provide a high amount of direct mental stimulation, as does interacting with other dogs at dog day care or on doggy play dates.

Another way to mentally stimulate your Whoodle is by teaching him a new command. Learning a new command or trick will stimulate his mind and help build the relationship and trust between you two, resulting in a generally more obedient and willing dog.

After your Whoodle has mastered all of the basic commands, get creative and teach your dog some fun tricks like jumping through a hoop, walking backward or crawling. You can even teach him to retrieve his toys by name then put them back in their designated places.

There are toys and puzzles designed specifically with mental stimulation in mind. Kong makes a range of toys that can keep your dog occupied for a long time and that are basically indestructible. A favorite is the "Classic Dog Toy." This is a rubber toy with a hollow center made for stuffing with treats. Kong has a safe line of treats and snacks or you can simply fill the toy with peanut butter. Kongs are dishwasher safe and cost between $8 and $25, depending on size, making them a great, affordable option.

Another way to keep your Whoodle mentally stimulated is with a dog puzzle. The Trixie Poker Box has four compartments all covered by a lid. Your dog must figure out how each lid can be removed to get the reward waiting inside. All four lids open differently so this will take some real focus and determination on your dog's part.

Keep in mind, once your Whoodle masters opening all boxes, this puzzle may not present a challenge anymore and he may become bored with it and uninterested, so keep the toy in your rotating arsenal for when your dog must be left alone.

If you prefer a mentally stimulating toy without the use of treats, try getting your Whoodle an Outward Hound Hide-A-Squirrel Puzzle Dog Toy. It's a hollow, plush tree stump with holes around it. Inside there are three plush squirrels that squeak. Your dog will have tons of fun trying to pull the squirrels from the stump. This is a great option for a dog who may need to watch his weight but probably isn't a good idea for a vigorous chewer as the squirrels are plush and may be torn apart easily by a determined Whoodle.

There are also electronic devices that you can control from a mobile device. Clever Pet is a unique system that challenges your dog with sequences, memory games and electronically released treats or food when solved. This system comes with a light-up pad that shows different colors and patterns. Clever Pet is designed to progressively get more challenging as your dog figures it out. Use the mobile application to track progress and monitor its use. This system is wonderful for dogs who are left alone for long periods. It comes with a $250 price tag but may be worth it if it means you don't have to spend money cleaning up after a bored, destructive dog.

If your Whoodle loves a game of fetch, check out the iFetch Frenzy. Not as high-tech as the original iFetch, which is electronic and can launch a tennis ball up to 30 feet, the iFetch Frenzy uses gravity instead of electricity to drop the ball through one of three holes and send it rolling across the floor. As long as your dog can learn to return the ball to the top, he can play solo fetch for hours while you are away.

Stories from a Whoodle Owner

The Swamp Dog

We live on a dirt road and, within a few weeks, Flynn had grown enough to need a longer walk than up and down the driveway. He was a January puppy, so there was lots of snow on the ground, and everything was well frozen when we first started our road walks. Soon, though, as he grew bigger, the weather warmed up and it became very obvious that our beautiful silky puppy was never going to be allowed on the furniture. Flynn had discovered the road-side ditches. With a single moment of inattention from us, on the other end of the leash, that lovely cuddly little ball of fur was proudly prancing through 3 inches of muddy slushy water. Flynn earned his nickname--Swamp Dog--at just a few months of age.

Some Whoodles love to swim. Flynn definitely thinks that swimming is for other dogs. He delights in racing up and down the shoreline of a freshwater lake or an ocean, splashing excitedly. If there are shorebirds to chase, it's even more fun. If we get into the water with him, and initiate a splashing game, he shoots right over the top of his excitement scale, splashing back. If we throw toys for him to fetch, he'll happily go after anything that doesn't require all four feet leaving the ground. If there's another dog fetching from the deeper water, Flynn waits for them to come back in, then happily chases dog and toy back to shore.

Flynn truly loves the water; it's just swimming that he disdains. So, we put a flotation jacket on him, and he rides around on the front of the paddleboard or whatever other boat is available, and we all enjoy ourselves. Luckily, we had bought a jacket that has a little chin support and a handle over the back, so if Flynn slides into the water, we just lean over and pick him back up.

Rotate Toys

When you have to leave your Whoodle alone for a while, rotate interactive toys that will help to keep him entertained while you are away. You may even leave the television on while you're gone. There are shows on DogTV that are geared specifically toward dogs that some pooches really seem to enjoy. This can be a great way to keep a talkative Whoodle distracted while you are away, especially for those who live in an apartment or townhome. A television program may also drown out any other noises that could get your dog barking while you are out.

Photo Courtesy of Lesha Hill

CHAPTER 9

Training Your Whoodle

Benefits of Proper Training

Training your Whoodle properly serves multiple purposes. Not only will it strengthen your bond together as you build a rapport, but it will also provide you a level of security while you are out together. A trained Whoodle will come when called. You should be able to trust that your dog will understand, stay, and obey in stressful situations. That obedience may even save his life in an emergency.

Photo Courtesy of Stacey McCumiskey

Training an intelligent dog such as a Whoodle can be simple yet challenging at times. The intelligence that makes them quick learners may also give them a stubborn edge to play by their own rules at times. Patience and determination are key.

There are options when it comes to obedience training. You can search local advertisements and attend a group class, hire a personal trainer to come to your home, or train your dog yourself. No matter what option you choose, be diligent with the training and stick to the schedule. The rewards of an obedient Whoodle will pay off for the rest of his life.

Training Your Whoodle at Home

Before you decide on the right path to training for you and your dog, there are a few things you need to consider. If you can't make it to obedience classes regularly then a personal trainer who can come to your home may be the best option. This choice can also keep your Whoodle safe from any viruses that may possibly be lurking at a training facility that hosts many dogs each week. This is an important factor to consider if your dog is young or vulnerable for any reason.

One drawback to training at home is a lack of distractions. In real-world situations, there will be noise, people, other pets and potentially many other distractions to steal your Whoodle's attention. In a group class setting, your dog is learning to be obedient regardless of what is going on around him and this is an invaluable skill that can keep him and you safe in dangerous or critical situations.

If you choose to train at home, remember to still regularly take your dog outside of your home to practice obedience with real-life distractions. If you hire a trainer, ask them how they are making sure to train your dog in all situations and about the possibility of taking a training field trip to a public place. This option gives you the best of both worlds with flexibility while also ensuring proper training.

If you are training a young or immune-compromised Whoodle and cannot risk exposing him to outside elements yet, consider practicing obedience in your own backyard or on your apartment balcony so he can at least be exposed to the sounds of nature while he trains.

Do-It-Yourself Training

If you choose to train your Whoodle alone, without the help of a trained professional, do your research before you begin. There are many resources, many of them free, to help you get a basic knowledge and understanding before you dive in. These resources include various books, online articles and YouTube videos that will help you understand methodology and step-by-step instructions.

When training at home, keep the sessions short, no longer than 15 minutes at a time so that your dog does not become frustrated or bored. Studies show that longer training sessions can actually cause your dog to retain less of what you are teaching.

Stories from a Whoodle Owner

Willow

Mixing up Training = More Whoodle Fun!

Willow learned all the basics in five sessions of puppy class, among them, Look, sit, stay, come, down and turn. (We're still working on drop it and leave it, but that's another story.) Willow is so smart, she mastered everything immediately and it became way too easy for her to earn her treat. Somehow, we had to make it more challenging.

We came up with a wonderful game. We put her on her 30-foot leash and take her into a wide-open area. Any space will do: local park, backyard or parking lot. And for 10 or 15 minutes, we have a blast. With treats in hand, we ask Willow to run between us, sit, stay, come, down and turn, all in different order, moving to different locations. This is an enormously fun game for her. Shaking up the commands and adding to them make it more challenging. She really has to listen, think and act accordingly before she gets her treat.

Know What to Expect – Obedience Classes

Regardless of your training method, have clear expectations so you know what to expect when training begins. You play as big a role in obedience training as your dog does, even if you don't do the training yourself. Properly training your Whoodle will take a significant time commitment and much dedication on both your part and his. Don't worry, it is worth it!

Obedience classes, private or group, are typically held once or twice a week. A good place to find one is by checking with your trusted vet or groomer for recommendations. They probably know quite a few and can recommend the best. You can also check local listings or find classes at your local pet store. Before deciding on one, check reviews and feedback for each program.

Most facilities require you to provide vaccination records before classes begin. Obedience training typically begins at about six months of age, but the ages of the doggy participants can vary greatly. It is never too late to begin obedience training, so even if you have adopted a senior Whoodle, he's not too old to learn.

Before your first training session, ask for a list of materials you will need to bring. The facility will likely require your dog to have a leash and may ask you to provide your own training treats. Most obedience classes require a name tag with identification and some require a clicker. Purchase all supplies ahead of time and be prepared for class so you are not wasting time with the trainer scrambling to get what you need.

No matter how often your Whoodle attends classes, be prepared to spend at least 10 to 15 minutes a few times a week reinforcing what your dog has learned. Just like any skill, obedience training takes practice and repetition.

Photo Courtesy of Emily Kowalchick

Basic Commands

Obedience training is not just about learning to sit or shake. It is about building trust between you and your Whoodle and learning to communicate effectively in a way your dog can understand. This trust begins by teaching your dog basic commands.

Most obedience classes or personal trainers will begin by teaching a few easy, basic commands. These commands lay the foundation for more complicated tricks later. If you are choosing to be the trainer yourself, remember to keep the training sessions short and positive so your dog does not get frustrated or bored. Follow the steps below to master these five basic commands.

LOOK - This is a basic building block to all other commands. Teaching your dog to "look" on command will allow you to hold his attention to teach him other skills and also allows you to command your Whoodle's attention in a situation where dangerous distractions may occur.

1. To teach this command, begin by holding a treat in front of your dog's nose and pulling it slowly up to your own forehead.
2. Say "watch me" or "look." Your dog should be staring at your forehead, awaiting the treat.
3. Praise him with a verbal "yes" and reward him with the treat.
4. Continue this a few times then begin the same process without a treat in your hand.
5. Continue to reward your Whoodle with a treat as he obeys the command with an empty hand.

Photo Courtesy of Erin Mossop

SIT – The sit command is the easiest one to teach and can be learned in a short period of time. Take your Whoodle to a calm area free of distractions. It's okay to have a little noise in the background. Have a bag full of very small training treats ready.

1. With your dog standing, facing you, hold a treat in front of his nose and slowly raise it up and over his head so he is forced to sit down and look up.
2. Give the verbal command "sit" as you do this.
3. When your Whoodle sits, reward him with a treat and a key phrase such as "yes" or "good." If you're training with a clicker, also give a click when your dog obeys the command.

DOWN - Once your Whoodle has mastered the sit command, move to the down command.

1. Guide your dog into a seated position, facing you.
2. Hold a treat in front of his nose, lower it to the floor, and give the verbal command "down."
3. If your dog raises his backside to a standing position to retrieve the treat, take the treat away and calmly say "no." Begin again from a seated position.
4. When your dog successfully lies down to retrieve the treat, reward with a treat, a positive verbal cue such as "yes" and a click.

Photo Courtesy of Megan Haggerty

HEEL – Teaching your Whoodle to heel requires him to walk on your left side at your pace whenever you're out and about. The heel command is a bit challenging and requires significant focus from your dog. He must stop when you stop and walk when you walk, never stepping in front of your left heel. This command is great for preventing leash tugging.

1. Begin by having your Whoodle sit in front, facing you.
2. Using your left hand, let your dog smell the treat then swing your arm around to the left, luring your dog to turn around and stop in a position next to you but slightly behind, facing the same direction you are.
3. Reward your dog immediately when he arrives in the correct position. Use the command "heel" as he comes into the correct position.
4. Repeat this process many times, always having your dog come to the heel position before rewarding him.

After your dog has mastered the heel position, progress by taking a few steps using the same verbal "heel" command. Reward your dog for walking with you in the correct position. If your dog leaves this position, guide him back to where he is supposed to be before continuing.

STAY/ COME – This is an important skill for a Whoodle who loves to chase or gets distracted by things while out. Good recall keeps your Whoodle safe when something unexpected grabs his attention, potentially luring him on a chase.

1. To teach your Whoodle to stay, command him to sit, facing you.
2. With a visible treat in hand, hold up your palm to your dog and say "stay." Take one step backward.
3. If your dog doesn't move, quickly return to your dog and reward him. You don't want your dog leaving the stay position to retrieve the treat.
4. If your dog moves, say "no" and return him to a sitting position. As your dog gets the hang of "stay," increase the number of steps between you and him.

LEAVE IT – This command is invaluable and can help keep your Whoodle safe if he gets into something potentially dangerous.

1. Begin with two treats, one in each hand. Keep one hand in a fist but allow your dog to sniff the treat.
2. As your dog tries to get into your hand to get the treat, verbally command him to "leave it."

3. Repeat this command until your dog backs off then reward with the treat from the other hand.
4. As your dog progresses, make the treat more accessible and challenge your pup to leave it in exchange for another treat.

DROP IT – This is another important command that can keep your Whoodle out of danger by telling your dog to drop something he has in his mouth. Teaching this command is similar to the "Leave It" command.

1. Begin by giving your dog a toy or other object to hold in his mouth. Command your dog to "drop it" and offer him a treat. Most likely, he will release the toy and take the treat.
2. Repeat this a few times with the treat visible then transition to giving your dog the verbal command to "drop it" without showing him the treat. When he drops it, reward him with the treat and verbal praise.
3. Make sure to give a strong, yet cheerful "drop it" before the treat is seen so your Whoodle will associate the command with the action.
4. As your Whoodle begins to get the command down, switch up toys and objects to practice with. Slowly mix in verbal praise as a singular reward instead of giving treats every time.

TURN – Turn is a very important command for Whoodles as they are known chasers. This command will recall your pup if he becomes distracted while out.

1. Walk your dog as normal.
2. Stop suddenly.
3. Command your Whoodle to "turn," then you should start walking backwards.
4. As he turns to follow your change in direction, reward him with a training treat.

NO JUMPING - Jumping is a common issue with Whoodles as they are easily excitable and energetic. For more information on training your dog not to jump, see the section on greeting new people in Chapter 7.

Training Methods

There are two main methods when it comes to training a dog: alpha-dog training and positive reinforcement. Hotly debated among trainers, these two methods are vastly different. When choosing the method that is right for your Whoodle, take all things into consideration after getting a firm understanding of the details of each.

Alpha Dog Training

Alpha training, popularized by dog trainer Cesar Milan, focuses on making you the alpha or the leader of the pack. This training begins early by maintaining heavy control over your dog's actions. Users of this method are told to never allow your dog in your bed, not to let a dog go through a doorway before you do and never to get down at eye level with your dog. It

Photo Courtesy of Adriano Magesky

is also advised that you touch your dog's food to get your scent on it before giving it to him and don't let him eat until you give the verbal okay.

Proponents of this method claim that dogs are pack animals and need to have a sense of who is in charge to learn to submit. They claim that wolves will assert their dominance over one another to keep each other in check. In reality, research has shown that wolves in the wild do not have such a rigid hierarchy. They live socially among each other much like humans do with our own families.

When it comes to obedience training, alpha training employs the use of restraints, such as choke and shock collars, and forceful body maneuvers. This method relies heavily on punishments and teaching your dog what he is doing wrong rather than teaching him how to do it right. While some trainers believe in the effectiveness of alpha training methods, others believe it is cruel and can actually undermine your relationship with your dog, making it one based on fear and not trust.

DANGERS OF CORRECTING BY PUNISHMENT

Alpha training employs the use of correcting by punishment, which has no scientific research backing it up as a legitimate training method. This type of forced control over a dog can lead to fear and anxiety in any dog breed, especially in a companion dog like a Whoodle. Using this method without an experienced professional's supervision can lead to a damaged relationship with your dog and a significant and sometimes permanent loss of trust.

Not only is this type of training risky and potentially dangerous, it is also often ineffective. Your dog almost never does anything "bad" intentionally. Almost always, your Whoodle will be aiming to please. If he is disobedient, it is most likely because he has not been taught what he is supposed to do.

When you punish your Whoodle for doing something undesirable, he will most likely only be hurt and confused by what has happened. He may never understand which action was the reason for his punishment in the first place and therefore won't know how to correct it.

Rather than punishing your dog for doing the wrong thing, show him what he is supposed to do, as discussed in the section on positive reinforcement, and reward him for that. It may take a little time to master but your relationship with your Whoodle will grow positively in the process and the effects will be long lasting.

Positive Reinforcement

> **HELPFUL TIP**
> **AKC Canine Partners**
>
> 
>
> Whoodles may not be an AKC-recognized purebred breed, but that doesn't mean that they can't participate in some of AKC's events. The AKC Canine Partners program is designed for hybrid and mixed-breed dogs. Enrollment in this program allows your dog to participate in certain AKC sports and events, such as Obedience and Agility. The program also includes optional pet insurance and a complimentary visit with a vet through the AKC Veterinary Network. All dogs are welcome! For more information about this program, visit the American Kennel Club website (www.akc.org).

The most effective and highly recommended method of training is positive reinforcement. This method reinforces good behavior and obedience with positive affirmation and treats while still letting your dog know you are in control. Bad behavior is not punished by harm or discomfort, rather it is ignored or redirected until the positive behavior is consistent.

Dogs have been selectively bred over thousands of years to live alongside humans. Dogs, especially "designer" dogs bred for companionship like the Whoodle, thrive on relationships and generally want to please their people. Positive reinforcement teaches them to understand what you want them to do and what makes you happy. The result is a positive owner-dog relationship that makes your Whoodle happy as well. Loyalty and trust naturally result from this style of training.

PRIMARY REINFORCEMENT

Primary reinforcements are directly related to innate, basic needs. This includes things such as food and water. Training treats (food) are a primary reinforcement tool successfully used in training.

SECONDARY REINFORCEMENT

Secondary reinforcements are things not based on instinctual, basic need but rather are cultural constructs. This includes smiles, pats and verbal praise. Your dog will learn to associate these actions positively when they are paired with primary reinforcements.

Another type of secondary reinforcement is conditioned reinforcement. This is when something neutral, such as a whistle or a clicker, is used in conjunction with a primary reinforcement to create a positive association. Conditioned reinforcements can be highly effective initially but can lose their effectiveness when the primary reinforcement is taken away for an extended period of time.

The E-collar Debate

E-collar is short for electronic collar, also known as a shock collar. These collars send a signal to your dog with a vibration, beep or electric shock controlled by either a remote or a fence. As with many training tools and methods, there are some who believe e-collars are both humane and effective and there are some who believe they should not be utilized in any situation.

While e-collars are typically used within the alpha training method, there are some who believe they can be used safely and effectively while training using the positive reinforcement method as well.

According to CanineJournal.com, electronic collars were first used in the 1960s to train hunting dogs. Today, these collars are used mostly to curb unwanted behaviors, such as barking, food aggression and straying beyond a designated area without a fence, also known as boundary training.

The collars work by emitting a beep or a vibration as a warning then delivering a shock to your dog if the behavior is not corrected. Depending on which brand you are using, your e-collar may come with varying levels of intensity, allowing you to begin with a very light shock.

In the opinion of some, e-collars may be utilized in very serious situations, to prevent the dog from a behavior that has potential to cause him serious harm. If you choose to do so, it should only be employed as a last resort and with the blessing of your trusted vet and trainer. E-collars have the potential to be inhumane and cruel if they are not used properly.

When to Hire a Trainer

If you are training your Whoodle at home but aren't seeing the progress you hoped for, it may be time to hire a professional. Frustration and confusion can send your dog mixed messages and cause major setbacks in the process.

If your Whoodle is dealing with any aggression or poor social behaviors that don't seem to be improving with work, hire a trainer specialized in that aggression to help you get it under control as quickly as possible. Make sure that any trainer you hire only uses positive reinforcement methods. A reputable and trustworthy trainer should have many previous clients willing to testify to a positive experience.

CHAPTER 10

Traveling with Your Whoodle

We all love the idea of taking our favorite companions everywhere we go, but traveling can cause your Whoodle unneeded stress. Should you bring your Whoodle along for the journey or leave him in a safe place while you are away? This chapter will explain the ins and outs of traveling with your Whoodle so you can make the best decision for you and your dog. For more information on specifically traveling with your dog by car, see Chapter 4.

Flying with Your Dog

Even if your Whoodle is small and it seems easy to let him tag along, flying with your dog requires a great deal of planning and preparation.

If your Whoodle is very small, it is possible your dog may be able to board the plane with you in the cabin. Typically, the weight limit for riding in the cabin is 20 pounds, though all airlines have different rules and they are constantly changing. It's best to check directly with the airline before purchasing your ticket.

Flying with your dog won't come cheap. Most airlines charge a pet fee of anywhere from $100 to $125 each way. Depending on the airline, your pup may have to fit into a small, well-ventilated carrier that fits below your seat by your feet for the duration of the flight and will not be allowed in your lap. Again, check specifically with your airline for these regulations as they all vary slightly.

Due to the size of a standard and typically even a mini Whoodle, your dog will most likely not be allowed to fly in the passenger area but instead will have to be checked in a crate into the cargo area. If at all possible, get a direct flight so your dog doesn't have to be transferred from aircraft to aircraft. No matter how much airlines have worked to improve the process for animals, air travel will still be traumatizing for your dog.

Each airline will have slightly different parameters for what you can and cannot put in your dog's crate on a flight. Most airlines will allow you to include a small bag of food that will be used in case of a delay or diverted flight. Some also allow drip style water dispensers for your dog to use during the flight. It may be a good idea to let your dog practice with one of these before the flight if he is not familiar with them. Most airlines also allow a small blanket or piece of clothing in the crate with your dog to provide a comforting scent of home.

Photo Courtesy of Bethany McCue

Among the things not allowed in the crate by most airlines are blankets or crate pads thicker than three inches, toys, bones or treats, any collars other than a flat collar and shredded newspaper, straw or hay bedding. Shock collars, metal collars, muzzles and medication for your pet are also prohibited. Remember, each airline is different and will have slightly different guidelines. Be sure to check specifics of your airline before your travel date.

Because there are only so many pets allowed on each airplane (this varies by airline and size of the plane), book your flight as early as possible to obtain a spot. In the past, airlines treated cargo animals just like any other luggage. Dogs were often left traumatized and sometimes even died because of high or low temperatures, lack of water, etc. Luckily, today, airlines have begun enforcing regulations to keep animals housed in the cargo area as safe and happy as possible. However, there is still some risk involved and you need to do your due diligence to make sure the airline you choose has a good reputation for keeping animals safe.

Not all airlines follow the same guidelines for flying animals. Some require a certificate of veterinary inspection (CVI) and certain vaccines before flying. Make sure you do thorough research on each airline before deciding on the best for you and your Whoodle. Federal regulations prohibit any pets under eight weeks old from flying.

Emotional Support Dogs

Until a recent FFA rule change, it was possible for your Whoodle to fly in the cabin with you as long as he was registered as an emotional support dog. This simply required a letter to the airline in advance of the flight. Recent rule changes have deemed that only certified service dogs performing a task or benefit for a disabled person will be allowed in the cabin during a flight. This means emotional support dogs no longer qualify as service dogs on airplanes.

Traveling by Train, Bus or Taxi

If you are planning to travel by train, bus or car service, it is important to know the guidelines for pets beforehand. If you are interested in train travel, Amtrak allows pets up to 20 pounds (including the weight of the carrier) but

Photo Courtesy of Erin Mossop

only on trips of 7 hours or less. If you are planning a bus trip with a major company like Greyhound, plan to leave your Whoodle home because animals are not allowed unless they are certified service animals.

If you are planning to utilize a car service, for your whole trip or even after a flight, make sure you notify them ahead of time that you have a dog with you. Legally, Uber drivers can deny you service if they are not made aware of pets in advance.

Hotel Stays with Your Dog

Not all hotels are pet friendly and some have size and breed restrictions. Before booking, call the hotel to be sure dogs are allowed. Even if their website states "pet friendly," call and double check that your specific breed and dog will be allowed. This can save a major headache when you get to the front desk and realize there was a mistake and your dog cannot stay. Checking online for the highest rated pet-friendly hotels is a great place to start.

When deciding on a hotel, consider how much outdoor space will be available to your Whoodle. Even some pet-friendly hotels offer very little in the way of pet amenities. Although your Whoodle doesn't need much outdoor space to do his business, he will need a place to exercise and expend a bit of energy safely.

Requesting a room on the ground floor, if available, will make it less of a hassle to take your dog outside to relieve himself. Middle-of-the-night potty breaks are much easier when it is just a short walk to a grassy area.

Some hotels are known for designating older, outdated or smoking rooms as pet rooms. Before booking, call and ask if

Soft-coated Wheaten Terriers, one-half of your Whoodle's genetic makeup, originated in Ireland hundreds of years ago and are considered to be the oldest Irish breed of Terrier. The true origin of this dog is shrouded in the mists of time, but the legend goes that a large blue dog swam ashore from a shipwreck off the west coast of County Kerry in Tralee Bay 200 years ago. This dog became known as the Wheaten Terrier and was valued for its skill in fighting. Whoodles are a much more recent addition to the Wheaten Terrier line, originating in the late 2000s or early 2010s. Understanding the rich history of the Whoodle's parent breeds is an excellent way to learn more about your dog!

the pet rooms are any different from other rooms so you know what you are paying for and what to expect.

Some hotels don't allow pets to be left alone, so make sure you check beforehand if you plan to leave your Whoodle there for a short time. Always bring a crate when staying in a hotel just in case. Even if you don't plan on using it, you never know when something might come up, and you don't want your dog to cause damage in the room if he must be left alone. Bringing an interactive toy such as a Kong may also help keep your Whoodle occupied and prevent barking while you are away.

Airbnb and VRBO

Another good option to explore is Airbnb and VRBO. There are many options that allow pets, but also many that do not. When searching for a place to stay, be sure to filter only rentals that allow pets of your Whoodle's size. It may be smart to call and double check before booking just to make sure there is no confusion before you arrive.

Dog-Sitters

Photo Courtesy of Abby Pruczinski

After evaluating the pros and cons of travelling with your dog, you may decide it is best to let him stay in someone else's care while you are away. Luckily, there are several choices for care while you are gone. If your trip is relatively short, hiring a dog-sitter may be an affordable option. This is when you hire someone to come and take your dog out 2 to 3 times a day and make sure he has food and water. Find a sitter through online resources such as petsitter.com, or ask a reliable friend or relative to do this. This is only a good option for very short periods as your dog will probably become anxious and bored without much company for more than a day or two.

You can also hire a 24-hour dog-sitter who will stay overnight to care for your dog. This will, of course, be a more expensive option. It allows your dog to have companionship and constant care, however, if he is particularly needy in that area.

Photo Courtesy of Nicolette Tosner

Boarding Facility

Much like hotels, each dog boarding facility is different and comes with its own unique amenities and policies. They range from small, cage-like kennels to large rooms with elevated beds and personal televisions. Some even have access to a doggy door that leads directly to a patio or an outside play area.

Many vets will board dogs as well, but they usually keep them in kennels all day except to let them out for potty breaks and maybe a short walk. For a better experience for your dog, find an independent dog boarder with a good reputation. They will have much more time to dedicate to your dog's social and emotional needs while you are away.

Most nice boarding facilities have a common area for dogs to run and play. Ask the facility how much time your dog will be allowed out to play so you can be sure he won't be stuck in his kennel or room all day. Price can vary drastically depending on location and amenities at each facility, but can range between $20 and $100 a night.

Never take your dog to a boarder that does not require the Bordetella vaccine. These places can be a breeding ground for kennel cough, so make sure you plan for your dog to get the vaccine at least two weeks before his visit.

When searching for the perfect place, begin by asking your local pet store or vet to see which they do and don't recommend. Most facilities charge a price per night and will often have different levels of service. Oftentimes, these places will allow you to choose between a private or shared room, and some have televisions with DogTV. Sometimes, you are even able to watch a live stream of your Whoodle while he is playing with his new dog buddies. You will probably pay extra for that peace of mind, however.

Photo Courtesy of Brent Boyle

If you don't want to hire a dog sitter or to take him to a boarding facility, you can also ask a responsible family member or friend to care for your Whoodle while you are away.

Whichever route you choose for your dog while you are away, choose an option that will allow you to be confident that your dog will be well cared for and happy in your absence. The last thing you want is to be worried about your Whoodle's well-being while you are on your trip.

Special Tips and Tricks for Traveling

No matter how far you are going, whether it's down the street or across the country, use these tips to help any trip with your companion be a stress-free one.

- Don't feed your dog within four hours of any trip. This includes car rides, plane rides and any other method of transportation. This may help save you from having to clean up vomit.
- Exercise your Whoodle vigorously a few days before and the day of your trip. Let him get as much energy out as he possibly can before being put into his carrier for the journey.
- Don't sedate your dog! This once common practice is no longer recommended by veterinarians. Sedating a dog can inhibit his ability to react in an emergency and is not good for his health.
- Check in as late as possible at the airport so that your dog doesn't have to spend the extra time waiting.
- If you are flying, make sure that your rental car or car service allows for dogs to ride.
- Always have a bowl, leash, water and plastic waste bags with you. No matter how you are traveling, these basic items will be daily necessities. If you're driving, use a safety harness as discussed earlier and stop often to let your dog go potty and drink water.
- Always have the number to a local emergency vet on hand. Emergencies can happen anywhere, so look up local animal hospitals before you travel—just in case!

CHAPTER 11

Grooming Your Whoodle

Coat Basics

The Whoodle coat is a combination of the soft, silky Wheaten coat and the curly poodle coat. Neither of these parent dogs shed, so the Whoodle should possess a very low to no shedding coat as well. Because the Whoodle is a cross breed and there is no standard for appearance, their coats will vary a bit from dog to dog, however, most Whoodles have a long to medium length wavy coat.

There are three basic coat types that your Whoodle may possess:

CURLY – A Whoodle with a curly coat has inherited more of a Poodle-type coat.

STRAIGHT – A Whoodle with a straight, silky coat has taken on more of the Soft-coated Wheaten Terrier characteristics.

WAVY – The most common Whoodle coat, wavy coats are a result of the combination of the two parent coat types, straight and curly.

Regardless of your Whoodle's coat type, this chapter will take you through all the grooming basics you need to know.

Basic Grooming Tools

In order to properly care for your Whoodle's coat, you will need a few basic care tools. With just a set of brushes, scissors, shampoo and detangler, you will have all you need to keep your Whoodle's coat healthy and beautiful.

If you choose to clip your dog at home instead of taking him to the groomer, which is an option we will discuss later in this chapter, you will also need to invest in a quality set of dog clippers. Aside from coat care, you will also need to have nail trimmers, styptic powder, a dog toothbrush, toothpaste, and ear and eye wash.

Brushing

Your Whoodle has high grooming needs and will need to be brushed a minimum of 4 to 5 times a week in order to prevent matting and keep a healthy coat. Bathing should only be done about once every 4 to 6 weeks. If you bathe your Whoodle too often, you will strip the oils from his skin which can lead to dryness and skin problems.

When it comes to grooming brushes, the options can become overwhelming. Each brush is created for a specific coat type and purpose so it can be a challenge to know which one is right for your dog. Because

Photo Courtesy of Amy Miller

Photo Courtesy of Joanne Gee

Whoodles can easily be prone to matting, a slicker brush is a necessity. These are usually flat with short, fine wire bristles. This brush should be used regularly to prevent mats. When using the slicker brush, make short, controlled movements to avoid causing breakage and static. Make sure you get the brush all the way to the hair shaft at the skin.

You will also want to purchase a natural bristle brush as a finishing brush. These brushes have tightly packed natural bristles and help to stimulate the skin's oils, keeping your dog's coat shiny and healthy. Give your Whoodle a once-over with this brush after using the slicker brush.

Bathing

When it comes to bathing, use a blow dryer to blow any excess dirt or hair off your Whoodle's coat before you begin. Keep the dryer far enough off the coat to avoid causing tangles and/or burning your dog's skin.

When shampooing your Whoodle, a safe, quality shampoo is a must. Ask a trusted vet or groomer what they recommend. Never use human shampoo or conditioner on your dog.

Any shampoo you use should be free from parabens, dyes, sulfates, and diethanolamine (DEA). These are ingredients commonly used in commercial shampoos but are known to have potentially damaging effects over time. It is also best to avoid any added fragrances, especially if your Whoodle has sensitive skin.

It is best to bathe your dog in a tub or sink, depending on his size, with a hand sprayer, but a large rinsing cup will do if that is all you have. Clean his coat all the way down to the roots, using your fingers to scrub and massage the skin. Rinse with cool water then use a towel to blot dry. Don't use the towel to rub your dog dry because this will cause tangles and mats to form in his coat.

Apply a quality detangler and finish drying with a hairdryer, using the same precautions to prevent tangles and burning as mentioned before. Use the bristle brush to remove any tangles that have occurred. Once finished, check the consistency of the coat with your hands. If one area feels denser, there are probably mats there. Go back over that area with the brush to remove them.

Detangling Spray

A good detangling spray can make grooming your Whoodle's mat-prone coat so much easier. When searching for a quality detangler, follow the same guidelines as when searching for a quality shampoo. Always avoid harmful ingredients!

Detangler can be used on wet or dry hair and works to loosen tangles and mats when used in combination with a brush. Apply after baths before brushing or even on dry hair before your Whoodle's regular brushing routine.

Stories from a Whoodle Owner

Winter Walks

Not only is Flynn a country dog, he is also a north-country dog. Winter comes early, and stays late, and particularly during those early season snow storms, and the lovely days of early spring when the snow is thick and soft, there is something about the Whoodle paw that leaves a lot to be desired. Snow clumps on every bit of long hair it comes into contact with when it is warm enough to be sticky (snowball-making snow), and it turns to ice when it clumps on the pad and between the toes. When temperatures drop into the teens and lower, the snow is too cold to bond to hair or even to a warm foot pad. But when the snow is fresh and the temperatures are in the high 20s or very low 30s, our lovely Flynn turns into a fair approximation of the abominable snow dog. Our walks become slow frustrating exercises that are not really much exercise, because Flynn stops every few minutes to chew the snow and ice out of his pads. On really bad days, he accumulates so much snow on his belly and lower legs that he can hardly move, and he sits down to chew that off too. This, of course, is self-defeating, because the more he chews and licks his hair and feet, the warmer and wetter these surfaces become, and as soon as he steps out, he accumulates even more snow than before.

It has taken us years to understand and judge the interactions of temperature and the age and type of the snow. Our language, unlike that of some native northern peoples, has only a few different words for snow. Whoodle owners need a word that says "this snow will stick!". In addition to learning to judge the conditions, we have had to learn what to do about it. Clipping the hair quite short between Flynn's toes and on his lower legs helps significantly, and so does applying special wax to his pads, the tops of his feet, and especially between the toes. There are products available for just this purpose, and I've seen recipes to make your own at home. We are careful to use a product that is safe to ingest, because if we're out long enough, eventually Flynn will stop and try to fix the situation himself by chewing off the accumulated snow. Any remaining wax goes with it, and it all ends up in his tummy. Of course the most frustrating part of the whole thing is that the worst conditions for your Flynn's feet are the most enjoyable for us to enjoy winter: it's not terribly cold, the snow is fresh and fluffy, and the trail is calling. Flynn is also eager to be out in these conditions, but even his enthusiasm is overcome when he becomes essentially encased in snow and can barely move as a result.

Nail Trimming

Most people opt to have a groomer or a veterinarian trim their dog's nails, but this is something that can easily be done at home. There are many styles of nail trimmers and which one you use is largely based on preference. Focus on ease of use and maneuverability. Most trimmers will come with instructions on how to clip the nails and it is important to follow them carefully to avoid injury to your dog.

A dog's nail is made up of the nail and the quick. The quick is the pink part inside the nail. If your dog has light-colored nails, the quick may be visible making it easier to avoid. If the nails are black, you will not be able to see the quick and will need to be extra cautious not to trim too far back. If you do hit the quick, this is a very painful experience for your dog. It will bleed a lot so immediately apply styptic powder.

The two most common types of nail trimmers are the guillotine type and the scissor type.

1. To use the guillotine or scissor trimmers, carefully place your Whoodle's nail into the clipper and cut at a 45-degree angle away from the pad.
2. The longer a dog's nails, the longer the blood supply is inside the nail, so only trim a little at a time, even if your dog's nails are overgrown.
3. As the nail is trimmed shorter, the blood supply will also retreat, making it possible to shorten your Whoodle's nails over time. Trim a small amount every 10 days or so until the nails are the length you want.

Your Whoodle may be a bit leery of the nail trimmers if he is not accustomed to having his nails cut yet. Introduce the trimmers to him early and often. Let him sniff and explore the trimmers while they are not in use so he can become comfortable before you attempt to trim his nails. Reward him with treats to create a positive association. Do this often, even when your dog doesn't need a nail trim. This will help him understand the trimmers are not a threat.

Cleaning the Ears and Eyes

You should clean your Whoodle's ears weekly in order to prevent infections.

1. Gently squeeze cleaning solution into one ear as directed on the bottle. You may need someone to help you hold your dog while you put the liquid in his ear.
2. Massage the ear canal then move on to the other ear.
3. Your Whoodle will shake his head afterward, which is normal.

You may also want to regularly flush your Whoodle's eyes if they are prone to catching dirt and debris. Use a dog eye wash and drop the recommended number of drops

HELPFUL TIP
Eyebrow Trimming

In between doggy haircuts, it might be necessary to give your Whoodle an eyebrow trim to prevent fur from blocking his vision. To give your Whoodle an eyebrow trim at home, first establish a calm environment and acclimate your dog to the sound and sight of scissors. Then follow these steps:

- Gently restrain your dog's muzzle; you don't want him to jerk his head and end up with a cut from your scissors! Always pause the trimming if your dog begins to squirm or look around.
- Comb the hair away from your dog's eyes.
- Allow your dog to smell the scissors.
- Trim the eyebrows with scissors pointed away from your dog's face

directly into the eye. Consult the directions on the bottle to know how often you should flush your dog's eyes.

Because a Whoodle has hair that continuously grows, much like humans, he will need regular haircuts around his face and eyes to keep his vision clear. Do this very carefully with a pair of dog shears or take your dog to the groomer every three weeks for a face trim. If you are unsure or nervous, take your dog to a professional groomer. Never attempt to trim the hair between a dog's eyes if your dog is upset and nervous. One wrong movement could cause serious injury to your Whoodle so you are better to be safe than sorry.

Dental Care

Your dog should be taken to the vet every year or two for a professional dental cleaning. Talk to your vet about how often he or she recommends. Dental health is often overlooked when it comes to dogs, but proper oral care is just as important for them as it is for us. Dogs can suffer from the same oral diseases and pains that humans do which sometimes can lead to debilitating pain and difficulty eating as your dog ages.

It is important to care for your dog's teeth at home by brushing regularly with a dog-specific tooth paste and brush. Due to the overwhelming number of older dogs with periodontal disease, some experts recommend brushing your dog's teeth as often as you brush your own, twice a day. Never use human toothpaste, which is full of additives that are meant to be spit out and not swallowed. Introduce the toothbrush to your Whoodle much like you did the nail trimmers, slow and easy.

When it comes to finding the right toothbrush for your dog, there are many to choose from. These include the standard one-sided bristle brushes with a handle, three-sided bristles designed to fit around your dog's teeth and clean all sides at once, brushes that fit over your finger and even sonic toothbrushes.

When it is time to brush, do it gently and slowly until your dog gets used to the sensation. You may want to begin with toothpaste on your finger if your dog is cautious about the toothbrush. Do this at the same time you brush him so he becomes accustomed to the routine.

1. Choose a calm time to introduce your dog to the teeth-brushing process.
2. Begin by gently touching your dog's teeth and gums before introducing the brush.
3. Add dog toothpaste to your finger and allow him to become accustomed to the taste and sensation.

4. As your dog becomes comfortable, introduce the brush with toothpaste. Take it slow and allow your Whoodle to become comfortable with it before pushing it on him to avoid resistance and fear.
5. Remember to praise your dog constantly as you are brushing his teeth. This is an unnatural experience for him and it may take some extra encouragement for him to become comfortable.
6. Reward with a treat after you are finished to provide positive association.

Brushing is not the only way to help your Whoodle keep his teeth clean. Chewing has been shown to naturally reduce plaque and tartar build-up. Dental chews come in many sizes, so just make sure you get the right size for your Whoodle, whether big or small. Keep a close eye on your dog to ensure that your precious pup does not try to swallow a piece that is too big for him and cause him to choke.

Photo Courtesy of Amanda Jaggers

Stories from a Whoodle Owner

Willow

The Teeth Brushing Battle

My husband brushes Willow's teeth every night after their evening walk. We've been told it's the single best thing we can do for her health on a daily basis and could possibly add several years to her life. As soon as they return from their outing, Willow knows what's coming. She will first try a distraction, hoping he will forget the nightly ritual, running around with a toy to engage him in a round of keep-away. Then she appeals to me for help. If I'm already in bed, she'll jump in next to me and get as close as possible, sometimes even sitting on me, in the hopes that I will protect her. Inevitably, my husband carries her off to the couch, while she makes the most horrible sounds of protest on earth. But eventually she settles down, realizes life is good and by the time he's done, she's usually sound asleep in his lap.

Anal Gland Expression

Dogs have anal glands, technically called anal sacs, that collect secretions within the sphincter muscles. The exact function of these glands is not entirely clear, but nonetheless, anal gland secretion is a must for all Whoodles.

While most dogs express anal gland secretions when they defecate, others have problems with secretion and need help. If your dog suffers from soft stool for any length of time, he may need help secreting his anal glands. If your dog is scooting on the floor or seems to be paying excessive attention to his rear end, this is a sign your Whoodle may need help expressing his anal glands. This can be done by a groomer or a trusted vet and should be a quick and painless process for your Whoodle.

Though most pet owners choose to have this done professionally, you can do this yourself fairly easily.

1. Place your fingers on each side of your dog's anus, slightly below and feel for small lumps that are the anal glands.
2. With a wipe or a paper towel, press and squeeze these glands up and together at the same time to express them.

3. A liquid will come out and can be wiped away with the towel or wipe you are using.

Although some veterinarians say anal expression should not be done manually unless your dog shows the signs of distress mentioned above, it is important to pay attention to his cues. Failure to express the anal glands can result in them becoming inflamed, impacted and even infected.

Your Whoodle will also need to be trimmed in the area of the anus every few weeks. If the hair is left too long, feces can cling to it and cause mats or even issues defecating if the mess is not resolved.

Cleaning your Whoodle's Paws

Keeping your Whoodle's paws clean before entering the house can be a challenge when there is wet weather outside. For those Whoodles living in cold climates, snow removal can be a challenge. Remove clumps of snow from your dog's fur by running slightly warm water over the snowy areas. Some people have also great success removing snow from fur using a common kitchen whisk to just brush it away.

Photo Courtesy of Annelies Morsink

For those days when paws get muddy, use paw wipes or similar products to spot clean your Whoodle so you don't have to give him a full bath. Mud Busters are also especially helpful for cleaning dirty paws. This is a cup with rubber bristles inside that help to scrub a muddy paw clean without making a mess.

Should I Clip at Home? When to Seek Professional Help

Keeping up with your Whoodle's regular grooming routine is very important for the health of his coat. He will need a full trim every 6 to 8 weeks. If you are not confident in your ability to trim his hair the proper way, seek professional help from a groomer.

While some may try to attempt the clippers at home, it is not as easy as a trained groomer may make it look. These at-home grooming sessions almost always take hours and ultimately end up back in the groomer to fix whatever went wrong. Save yourself time and effort and let the professional care for your dog's coat.

If you must trim your dog yourself, consider taking a class or lesson from a trained groomer so you can better understand your Whoodle's needs.

Choosing a Groomer

When choosing a groomer to care for your Whoodle, first ask friends and family whom they use for their dog's grooming needs. Personal recommendations are the best way to find a reputable groomer who cares for the

Photo Courtesy of Amy Rizer

dogs and produces quality cuts. Ask for photos of a groomer's work. If they cannot produce evidence of his work, find another groomer.

You may also check local reviews online. Call and request a tour of any places you're interested in so you can see firsthand how they care for the dogs. If cleanliness is not a top priority at a facility you visit, walk away and find another groomer.

Questions to Ask a Groomer

Before choosing a groomer, knowing what questions to ask will ensure you know exactly what you are getting . Here are some key questions to ask before bringing your Whoodle in.

HOW MUCH DO YOU CHARGE? Make sure you know exactly what it will cost up front. Sometimes, groomers will initially tell you their base fee but then surprise you with certain upcharges upon pickup. Be sure you know exactly what it will cost so there is no confusion.

HOW LONG WILL IT TAKE? If you have never taken a dog to the groomer, you may be surprised to discover that it can take several hours. It is not uncommon for a groomer to keep (or work on) your dog for four hours. Knowing how long it will take allows you to plan your day accordingly without interruption.

WILL MY DOG BE CRATED? Some groomers utilize crates to keep your dog safe while they are not being cut. If you do not want your Whoodle to spend time in the crate, you may want to arrange for the groomer to call you as soon as he is finished so you can pick your dog up as quickly as possible. Some groomers work on more than one dog at a time. These facilities typically keep your dog in a crate more often than groomers that work on one dog at a time.

DO YOU MAKE HOUSE CALLS? Some groomers, but not all, offer house calls. This can be especially useful for dogs who get nervous or exhibit anxiety about going to the groomer.

Whatever method of grooming you choose, do not neglect your Whoodle's grooming needs, or you may find that it can get out of hand quickly and will become a much bigger job. Matting leads to skin issues that may need veterinary care to resolve.

CHAPTER 12
Basic Health Care

Visiting the Vet

Regular vet care is crucial for the well-being of your Whoodle throughout his life. Puppies will need to receive several rounds of vaccinations during their first year of life, so be prepared for the cost before you bring your Whoodle pup home. After maturity, your adult Whoodle will only need yearly exams, barring illness or injury. Regardless of your Whoodle's age, always schedule a vet appointment within the first week of bringing him home. This applies to dogs purchased at pet stores, shelters and breeders. As discussed

Photo Courtesy of Kristen Londoño

in Chapter 2, most breeders will stipulate this initial wellness appointment in their contract.

Throughout his life, your Whoodle should see a veterinarian regularly for routine check-ups and vaccinations. At these routine appointments, your dog should get a thorough look over to make sure he is in good health. The vet will weigh your Whoodle, listen to your dog's heart and lungs and perform an ear, eye, nose, and mouth examination. The visit should also include an abdominal examination, looking for any abnormalities.

The veterinarian may also take a stool sample to check for parasites and draw blood to check for heartworms. He may examine your dog's gait and coat condition. Come prepared to answer questions about your Whoodle's diet and routine. Like most dog breeds, Whoodles are susceptible to a few genetic conditions. Staying up to date with wellness exams can help the vet catch any issues early.

Fleas

Fleas are the most common external parasite to afflict dogs and they are a problem almost everywhere. They reproduce quickly, as a single female flea can lay 20 to 40 eggs a day. If your dog picks up a flea or two from the park and he has not been protected, you could be dealing with an infestation in your home before you know it.

Flea prevention is very important for both you and your Whoodle's health. There are many options when it comes to prevention. Each has unique advantages and disadvantages, so it is important to do thorough research before making a decision.

Topical flea preventative is one popular option. This medication comes in a small tube that the owner squeezes onto the dog's back between the shoulder blades. This topical medication usually takes about 12 hours to take effect and will last about 30 days before it needs to be reapplied. The solution is absorbed into the skin and circulates through the dog's bloodstream, treating fleas and ticks over the entire body, not just the area it was applied.

One disadvantage of this application method is the greasy spot it leaves on your dog's back for a few days. Care must be taken to not touch this area or come into contact with the medication yourself as it will also absorb into your skin. This is especially important for children who may not be aware of the area the medication was applied.

There is usually a minimum age requirement for these medications, so it is best to consult your vet before applying topical flea treatments to a young dog.

Another method of administration is oral medication. There are many tablets on the market that prevent fleas and ticks for 30 days. Some of these are combination pills that prevent heartworms and internal parasites as well. This is a way to prevent parasites without the mess of topical medication.

Just as with any medications, side effects exist with these preventative pills. While they are generally mild, some dogs can react with skin irritations, vomiting or diarrhea. Consult your vet immediately if your dog has any ill effects after using an oral preventative.

Flea collars are another option. These collars are worn in addition to your dog's identification collar and are covered with topical flea medication, usually permethrin. These collars provide up to eight months of protection for your dog but are not risk-free. Flea collars can also cause skin irritation so look out for that if you choose to go this route.

While flea collars have been deemed safe for dogs, permethrin can cause toxicity in cats. Just like with topical medication, children and adults should avoid contact with the active ingredients on flea collars. Flea collars should never be used on a young puppy.

Even dogs that live primarily inside need to be on a flea and tick preventative. One trip outside is all it takes to pick up a flea or two that can cause an infestation. It is much better to take preventative measures than to have to deal with the fleas or ticks after they've hitched a ride into your home.

Fleas can infect your dog with tapeworm if he ingests one. Fleas can also cause an allergic reaction on your Whoodle's skin, which can lead to sores and shedding. If a flea infestation becomes very severe, anemia can occur. If your dog's gums or the insides of his eyelids appear pale or white, call the vet immediately to check for anemia.

Treating a Flea Infestation

If you suspect your dog might have fleas, there are a few things you can do to help get rid of them. First, skip the flea bath. These shampoos contain harmful chemicals that may cause irritation for your Whoodle. As these shampoos only kill the existing live adult fleas on your dog, leaving the eggs and larvae untouched, they are only a temporary solution that aren't worth the risk. Instead, use a mild dish soap such as Dawn to bathe your Whoodle. Nontoxic to your dog, this bath is both effective and safe for killing live adult fleas.

You can also purchase a flea comb at any pet store and use that to help you find the fleas on your dog's body. These have very fine and closely spaced teeth that fleas cannot pass between. Run the flea comb over your dog's body at a 45-degree angle, focusing on the head, neck, and hindquarters. If you see a flea in the comb, cover it quickly, trap it in a wet paper towel, and drop the flea in a bowl of soapy water to kill it.

Photo Courtesy of Char Simons

If you find fleas on your dog, you will need to vacuum every area from the floor to the curtains. Anything upholstered is potentially a place where a flea has laid eggs. If you notice fleas in your home, continue vacuuming twice a day for two weeks in order to get rid of all the fleas as they hatch. Once a flea infestation happens, it can be difficult to eradicate so be diligent as soon as you notice the problem.

Ticks

Ticks can go largely unnoticed by their host, but they can cause a much bigger health problem than fleas. Ticks are notorious for transmitting dangerous diseases to dogs, humans, and other animals. While most ticks will prefer your furry friend as a host, they also won't hesitate to latch on to you if given the opportunity.

Lyme Disease

Lyme Disease is the most common tick-borne disease in the United States of America. It carries serious risks for both humans and animals and should be treated promptly at the first sign. Transmitted by the black-legged tick, commonly known as the deer tick, this disease has been reported in every state, but is most prevalent in the northeast.

Lyme Disease can present with varying symptoms, but in humans often begins with a bull's eye–shaped rash appearing 3 to 30 days after the bite. If you experience this symptom, seek medical care promptly for treatment. Other signs of Lyme Disease are flu-like symptoms such as fever, chills, body aches, headaches and swollen lymph nodes. Most cases can be eradicated fully with antibiotics if caught early.

If you have been bitten by a tick and show symptoms of Lyme Disease, see a doctor even if your symptoms seem to resolve on their own. You may still have Lyme Disease and it can potentially spread to other parts of your body while undetected.

Lyme disease in dogs may present similarly. If you find a tick on your Whoodle, watch out for fever, weakness in limbs, joint swelling, loss of appetite, fatigue and general discomfort or pain. Lyme Disease can progress dangerously in dogs just as it can in humans, so prompt treatment with an antibiotic is required. If your vet suspects Lyme Disease, they will typically perform a C6 test to detect antibodies which indicate infection. Lyme Disease cannot be passed from an infected dog or human to another. It is only transmitted through the bite of an infected tick.

Photo Courtesy of Gretchen Berrocal

Depending on where you live, some veterinarians recommend the Lyme vaccine for dogs. Before you agree to get the jab for your Whoodle, know the risks. This vaccine is highly controversial and many people believe it does more harm than good. In fact, studies show the Lyme vaccine is less safe than any other canine vaccinations, showing more adverse reactions after 3 days. If you live in an area where Lyme Disease is prevalent, talk to your vet and determine if the Lyme vaccine is worth the risk for your Whoodle.

ANAPLASMA: Symptoms of anaplasma are terribly similar to Lyme Disease but can also include low platelets, usually detected by unusual bleeding or bruising. The bacterium causing anaplasma is typically found in the Northeast and upper Midwest United States and the western coastal states.

CANINE EHRLICHIOSIS: This tick-borne disease is found all over the world and is transmitted by several types of ticks. Symptoms of infection include loss of appetite, fever and low blood platelets. Take your Whoodle to the vet promptly for treatment at the first sign of infection to avoid chronic symptoms that are much more difficult to manage.

ROCKY MOUNTAIN SPOTTED FEVER: Another common disease to affect humans as well as dogs is Rocky Mountain Spotted Fever. Carried by a variety of ticks, it is found all over the United States as well as Central and South America. Signs and symptoms are similar to the others and include fever, loss of appetite, joint pain, low platelets, swollen lymph nodes and occasionally neurological signs.

BABESIOSIS : This disease can cause hemolysis, or a breakdown of red blood cells causing symptoms such as jaundice, pale gums, dark urine and lethargy, depression and sometimes enlarging of the spleen. This is a potentially fatal disease so seek veterinary care at the first sign.

Tick Prevention

Ticks are often treated by the same medications used to prevent fleas. Make sure your monthly flea preventative also protects against ticks to help your Whoodle avoid infection. Aside from medication, avoid tall brush or un-mowed grassy areas to prevent ticks from hitching a ride on your pup. If you do take your dog into an area with tall greenery, inspect him promptly when you return home. If you find a tick on your dog, remove it immediately following these instructions.

1. With gloves on your hands, use a clean pair of tweezers and grab the tick firmly as close to the skin as possible.
2. Pull firmly, straight up. You don't want to leave any of the tick's mouth-parts behind or this could lead to infection.
3. Once you have removed the tick, place it in a jar of alcohol or soapy water. Clean the bite thoroughly with antiseptic and watch the area for signs of irritation.
4. Keep the tick for identification in case your dog shows any symptoms of illness. Symptoms can take two weeks to surface, so watch your Whoodle carefully.

Take safety precautions seriously as you don't want to come into contact with the tick's saliva or risk being bitten yourself.

Although ticks and fleas are seasonal in many regions, most vets recommend keeping your dog on a preventative year-round to make sure he is always protected.

Worms and Parasites

There are a number of intestinal worms and parasites that can wreak havoc on your dog's health if left untreated. These include hookworms, ringworms, roundworms, tapeworms, whipworms, coccidia, giardia and spirochetes. A vet typically diagnoses these parasites through a stool sample, but there are particular symptoms you can watch for.

HOOKWORM – Hookworm larvae live in the soil and can be picked up by your Whoodle through common activities. These parasites attach themselves to the intestinal walls and feed off the dog's blood. As with most parasites, puppies are most susceptible to hookworms. Diarrhea and weight loss can be signs of possible hookworm infestation, which requires a vet diagnosis.

Once diagnosed, hookworms can be treated with an oral medication. Depending on the severity, iron supplements may be needed to treat anemia. Humans can also contract hookworms, often by walking barefoot on soil contaminated with feces. Symptoms include abdominal pain, intestinal cramps, nausea, fever, blood in stool and a rash. This is more common in developing nations as humans rarely contract hookworms in the United States.

RINGWORM – Ringworm is actually a fungus, not a worm, and it causes circular bald patches on your dog's skin. This condition is easily spread and mostly affects dogs with compromised immune systems, including young puppies and elderly dogs. Depending on the severity of the infection, your vet will likely treat your dog with a medicated shampoo and possibly an oral medication.

ROUNDWORM – Roundworms are extremely common in dogs and are usually discovered when an owner spots round, white worms, an inch or two in length, in a dog's stool. There are other symptoms to keep an eye out for, such as coughing, vomiting, diarrhea, and weight loss, however, these only present in severe cases. Roundworms can also be passed to humans, especially children.

TAPEWORM – A dog can get tapeworms when it accidentally ingests parasite larvae, often by eating a flea. Weight loss and diarrhea are common symptoms of tapeworm, as are small worm segments resembling grains of rice in your dog's stool. Treatment for tapeworms involves oral medication and sometimes injections as well.

WHIPWORM – Unlike other intestinal parasites, whipworms are difficult to spot in a stool sample. These worms live in the large intestine and cause weight loss in dogs. A sign of infection may be a mucous covering at the tip of your dog's stool. While whipworm infection is not typically serious, oral medication is required to eradicate them.

COCCIDIA, GIARDIA, AND SPIROCHETES – These are not worms but are single-celled parasites that can do much damage to your dog before you even know he is infected. These parasites can cause lasting diseases and issues for a dog and require swift treatment from a vet. Often transmitted through water, food, soil, and feces, these parasites live in unsanitary conditions. Young puppies and older dogs are more susceptible due to their weakened immune systems.

Medication to treat these parasites is typically given orally. The severity of the case will determine the length of time these medications will need to be taken.

HEARTWORM – While not an intestinal parasite, heartworms are much more severe. These worms are transferred via mosquito bite. If an infected mosquito bites your Whoodle, it takes about 6 to 7 months for the larvae to develop into adult heartworms. These worms live in your dog's heart and arteries and cause major issues, such as lung, heart and artery damage, that can last even after the worms are eradicated.

Treatment at the earliest sign is vitally important and can make the difference between a good outcome or bad. Early symptoms of heartworm disease in dogs include loss of appetite, persistent cough, fatigue and no motivation to play and exercise. As the disease progresses, symptoms become more severe and include bloating due to fluid build-up in the abdomen and even heart failure.

Heartworms are most common in the southern portion of the United States, especially the states around the Gulf of Mexico, however, it has been recorded in all 50 states. Most dogs should be taking a preventative medication beginning around the age of 6 months. There are several options including topical, oral and injection, depending on what area of the country you live in, so discuss preventative options with your vet to determine what is best for your Whoodle.

Your dog should be tested for heartworm yearly even if he's on a preventative to be sure it is working. Heartworm disease is very dangerous for your Whoodle and very difficult and expensive to treat, so the earlier you catch it, the better. If your dog is diagnosed with heartworm disease, treatment costs anywhere from $500 to $1,500 and isn't guaranteed to work. Never skip a month of preventative, it only takes one mosquito bite to cause serious damage down the road.

Vaccinations

Vaccinations are an important part of keeping your dog healthy and safe from potentially life-threatening illnesses. They prevent diseases by injecting the body with antigens to elicit an immune response producing antibodies for those diseases. The vaccinations cause no symptoms of disease but give the dog's body time to build up an immunity so that if the dog comes into contact with a virus, his immune system will respond fast enough to shorten the illness significantly.

A newborn puppy will first receive antibodies from its mother's milk for at least the first six weeks of its life and should be protected from many illnesses that way. Distemper, adenovirus, hepatitis, parvovirus, and parainfluenza are considered the core vaccinations that every puppy should receive when nursing ends, at about six weeks of age. These shots are usually given in four rounds: once at six weeks, 10 weeks, 14 weeks and 18 weeks.

Many vets administer these core shots in a combination vaccine called a 5-Way. Depending on your area, some vets may recommend additional vaccinations. These could include Bordetella, leptospirosis, and coronavirus (unrelated to COVID-19).

The rabies vaccine is always administered separately and is recommended no earlier than 12 weeks. Some veterinarians may want to give it in addition to other combo vaccinations at your dog's second-round appointment. Depending on where you live, legally, your dog must receive a rabies vaccine every one to three years.

Negative reactions to vaccines are rare but still possible. Sometimes vaccinations can trigger an allergic reaction causing swelling, hives, vomiting and fever. If your dog does have a reaction, notify your vet immediately. Even if the reaction is mild, make sure the vet is aware before your dog is given more vaccinations as symptoms could be the same or worse the next time. Overall, the benefits of vaccinations far outweigh the risks.

Oftentimes, but not always, vaccinations are required to access many dog-related facilities. These may include kennels for boarding or day-care, groomers and sometimes training facilities. Be sure to keep access of vaccination records in case you need to show proof.

Diseases and Conditions in Whoodles

Unlike purebred dogs, crossbreeds are typically less afflicted by severe genetic conditions. This means your Whoodle is set up to be a much healthier dog from the start! Although less likely to suffer from the genetic conditions that affect his purebred parents, he is still susceptible to some. It's important to understand the common diseases that can afflict Whoodles, so you can be prepared in any event.

ADDISON'S DISEASE – Addison's disease, also known as hypoadrenocorticism, results in decreased hormone production from the outer cortex of the adrenal gland. Symptoms of this disease are usually vague but may include lethargy, diarrhea, vomiting, increased thirst and urination, and weight loss. Shaking episodes also occur occasionally.

If your Whoodle is exhibiting any of these symptoms, Addison's disease should be considered. Once diagnosed, treatment involves lifelong injectable hormone replacement therapy, often accompanied by steroids. It may take a while to regulate your dog's hormone levels, so expect frequent visits to the vet for tests. Treatment for Addison's disease is typically successful and your dog should resume a normal and healthy life as long as treatment continues.

PROTEIN-LOSING NEPHROPATHY (PLN) AND PROTEIN-LOSING ENTEROPATHY (PLE) – These two protein-wasting conditions sometimes afflict Soft-Coated Wheaten Terriers and could affect a Whoodle. Caused by improper function of the kidneys, the afflicted dog loses blood serum and protein into the urine.

PLN symptoms include vomiting, loss of appetite, weight loss and difficulty urinating despite sufficient water intake.

PLE symptoms include decreased appetite, fluid retention and build up in the chest or abdomen, bloody diarrhea, vomiting and lethargy.

While these are serious conditions, both may be treatable with diet and medication if caught soon enough.

HIP DYSPLASIA – Hip dysplasia is a condition in which the ball and socket of the hip joint do not grow at the same rate. This disease is not usually diagnosed until the age of two. This abnormal formation causes a looseness of the joint which may lead to pain and even lameness. Hip dysplasia is not a life-threatening disease but can greatly reduce the quality of a dog's life. Sometimes, hip dysplasia can be managed with drugs, weight control and monitored exercise. However, a Whoodle with severe hip dysplasia may need surgery to attempt to repair or replace the hip altogether.

Photo Courtesy of Bethany McCue

PORTOSYSTEMIC SHUNT – This genetic disease is caused by an abnormality in the portal vein in the abdomen. This causes some of the dog's blood to bypass the liver and pump into the body, delivering toxins to major organs. Symptoms of the condition include loss of coordination, poor muscle development, vomiting, diarrhea, loss of cognitive function and excessive drooling.

This condition is diagnosed with a blood test. Once confirmed, surgery to repair the portal vein is the best option. Diet restriction and medications as prescribed by your vet may also help.

Though rare, this condition more commonly affects Mini and

Toy Poodles so if your Whoodle was bred from a smaller poodle, he may be more likely to be affected by this condition.

OTHER NOTABLE DISEASES – Whoodles may be affected by eye conditions, such as progressive retinal atrophy and entropion, an abnormality in which the eyelids roll inwards. Ear issues may also arise due to improper care from the hair growing inside. See chapter 11 for more information on ear care for Whoodles.

Immune disorders are also possible, including allergies, thyroid conditions, cancer, inflammatory bowel disease and other autoimmune disorders. It's also worth noting both the Poodle and Soft-Coated Wheaten Terrier are known to have sensitive stomachs, so this is something fairly common among Whoodles.

Holistic Alternatives and Supplements

Whether your Whoodle has developed a medical condition, or you are taking preventative measures, the first step toward a healthy lifestyle for your dog is proper diet and supplementation. Holistic alternatives have been used for centuries in place of medication or as preventative care to support wellness. Below are some alternative care methods becoming more commonly used on dogs.

Acupuncture

Acupuncture involves pricking the skin or tissues with needles. This practice is becoming more common in pets because of its notable benefits in managing pain and increasing circulation. Supporting overall wellness, acupuncture can aid in the treatment of hip dysplasia, allergies, gastrointestinal problems, and pain due to cancer treatments.

Acupuncture causes no pain and is shown to have a calming effect in pets. Though this is a promising alternative to medications, you should always consult your veterinarian before beginning any treatment. Acupuncture should only be performed by a certified acupuncturist.

Herbs

Herbs are a staple in holistic health care, however, not all herbs are safe for dogs. Some can interact with medications your dog may be taking and have detrimental effects. Discuss all herbs with your vet before adding them to your dog's diet or lifestyle. Some commonly used herbs include:

Goldenseal. Anti-inflammatory and anti-bacterial, goldenseal can be used externally on bodily infections or as an eyewash for infections or conjunctivitis. It can be taken internally at the first sign of kennel cough or digestive issues and can also be beneficial in the treatment of tapeworms and giardia. Goldenseal should not be used for too long as it can cause stress on the liver.

MILK THISTLE. Milk thistle provides liver support by protecting against damage. If your dog is on any medication that can damage his liver, discuss adding milk thistle to his regimen with your vet.

GINGER. Just as with people, ginger is an effective tool for treating nausea and cardiovascular conditions in dogs. Ginger has cardiotonic effects and can promote functionality of the heart.

CHAMOMILE. Another herb that aids digestion, relieves muscle spasms, and reduces inflammation, chamomile is a great option for treating chronic bowel and gas disorders and can also ease your Whoodle's anxiety.

LICORICE. Licorice root is a fast-acting anti-inflammatory that can be used to treat arthritis and other inflammatory diseases. It has been shown to enhance the efficacy of other herbs, so it is often combined with others as a part of a treatment plan.

CBD OIL. As per the American Kennel Club's website, "Currently, there has been no formal study on how CBD affects dogs. What scientists do know is that cannabinoids interact with the endocannabinoid receptors located in the central and peripheral nervous systems, which help maintain balance in the body and keep it in a normal healthy state."

CBD oil, also known as cannabidiol, is thought to treat pain and help control seizures in dogs. Anecdotal evidence also shows that CBD oil may have anti-inflammatory, anti-cancer, anti-anxiety and cardiac benefits. Discuss with your vet the option of adding a CBD supplement to your dog's lifestyle.

These are only a few of the herbs available for homeopathic use for your dog. If you want your dog to experience the benefits of herbal remedies but can't source the herbs yourself, there are many pre-made solutions and tinctures available conveniently packaged and mixed with directions. This can help ensure you are using the herb correctly.

Only use products from a source with a reputation for supplying the best holistic and herbal treatments. Beware of cheaper products that may contain synthetics. And always consult your vet before beginning any herbal treatment for your Whoodle.

Pet Insurance

Some pet owners choose to invest in pet insurance in the event any conditions arise. It is advisable to carefully research each provider to weigh costs versus benefits before taking out a policy. Each company offers different coverage, so be sure to read the fine print and understand any exclusions, however, there is almost always an annual deductible you must meet before insurance will cover any costs. Even after the deductible is met, the average policy pays only about 80 percent, with wellness exams and vaccinations not included. If you are considering pet insurance, your vet may be a good resource for information.

Insurance rates will vary based on your dog's specific age, history and condition. While it is generally considered more affordable to pay out of pocket for vet visits for common ailments, pet insurance can be a life-saver if something catastrophic arises. It can save you big if your Whoodle needs extensive tests or surgery or if he requires medication for life.

CHAPTER 13
Nutrition

Benefits of Quality Dog Food

Just as we know the importance of a well-balanced diet as humans, dogs need the same for optimal health and wellness throughout their lives. For the sake of our health, we do our best to eat a diet without processed foods or harmful additives. These same rules apply when it comes to feeding our dogs. Dogs also need a certain balance of protein, fats, carbohydrates, vitamins and minerals to stay healthy.

All commercial dog foods have been tested rigorously and are required to meet minimum nutritional requirements. However, minimum requirements

Photo Courtesy of Robin Feinman

are not what is best for your dog's health long-term. Feeding your dog low-quality food every day is the equivalent of you eating junk food every day. It does not promote or sustain optimal levels of health.

Choosing a dog food that is made with the best ingredients, without preservatives and additives, will help your dog function at his peak level, potentially protecting him against disease.

> **HELPFUL TIP**
> **Know Your Size**
>
> When choosing food for your Whoodle, it's important to consider which size your Whoodle's Poodle parent was. If the Poodle parent was a Miniature or Toy variety, you might want to opt for a food that is nutritionally formulated for a small-breed dog. If you don't know the size of your Whoodle's Poodle parent, you can choose dog food based on your pet's age and current size. When in doubt, talk to your vet!

According to Dr. Hugh Stevenson, a veterinarian in Ontario, Canada, for more than 20 years, symptoms of poor nutrition include a dull, thin coat, poor quality footpads (which can crack or bleed), weight problems, excess stool and gas and passing undigested grain particles in feces.

Quality dog nutrition leads to a lustrous coat, healthy skin and weight and less stool due to more of the food being digestible.

Providing your Whoodle with the best nutrition possible is a great way to keep him healthy.

Types of Commercial Dog Foods

Many dog foods on the shelf claim to be the best, healthiest and most complete. Some are dry, some are wet, and some are a combination of both, but they each have vastly different ingredients. Determining the right food for your Whoodle can be both confusing and overwhelming. When each bag or can contains a different list of ingredients and promises on the label, how do you really know what you're getting or what is best for your companion?

When it comes to choosing your dog's food, the first decision you will have to make is whether to feed your dog dry kibble or wet food. Dry and wet dog food each comes with its own set of positives and negatives.

WET DOG FOOD – One undeniable con of wet dog food is its very strong smell. While this may be a negative for you, it may actually be a positive for a dog who doesn't have much interest in eating. The strong scent may be enough to entice a picky Whoodle to eat.

Wet food also helps with hydration if you have a dog that doesn't drink as much as he should, but it spoils quickly after opening. If your dog doesn't finish his food promptly, you'll need to store the rest in the refrigerator. Canned food can also be a bit messier to eat, depending on your dog, and may get stuck in your Whoodle's beard or facial hair every time he eats.

DRY DOG FOOD – Unlike wet, dry dog food doesn't spoil when left out. This type of food may be beneficial for a dog who likes to nibble on his food throughout the day. Dry dog food also has minimal smell, so it can sit out without much notice. Some dry kibble is also formulated to help clean your dog's teeth while he chews, although some experts say the added grains in certain dry foods contribute to tooth decay.

Whichever type of food you choose for your dog, it's important to remember that both canned food and kibble exist in low-quality forms. Low-quality

Photo Courtesy of Piper Harris

brands include cheap fillers, artificial colors and flavors, and preservatives and should be avoided.

Dehydrated Dog Food – This dog food typically begins the dehydration process raw, so it is nutritionally similar to a raw diet. Proponents of dehydrated dog food claim that it has all the benefits of a nutrition packed raw diet with none of the risks. Dehydrating dog food allows it to be kept for up to 12 months safely without the use of preservatives. Because it isn't cooked prior, it retains more nutrients than other dry options. Freeze-drying is another way to produce dehydrated dog food with the same benefits.

RAW FOOD DIET – While homemade raw food is risky and potentially dangerous for you and your Whoodle, there are now several companies that sell raw food options in the refrigerated pet food section. Discuss the pros and cons of a raw food diet with your vet because it is highly controversial. While some tout incredible health results, others claim that long-term, a raw food diet can lead to health issues due to an unbalanced diet.

Ingredients to Watch Out For

Dog food ingredient lists can be confusing and tricky to understand. Companies that produce low-quality dog food tend to use vague terms and scientific words to trick the consumer into thinking the product contains quality, wholesome ingredients, when it may not. Below is a list of key ingredients to avoid when searching for the best commercial dog food for your Whoodle.

BHA/ BHT – Studies are not conclusive, but these chemical preservatives have been linked to hyperactivity and cancer. Used to preserve fats in human food and pet food, BHA and BHT have been banned in some countries but are still allowed in the United States, Canada and Europe. Until conclusive evidence proves these preservatives are safe, it's best to avoid them altogether.

MEAT, MEAT MEAL OR RENDERED FAT – Any time you see a vague, non-specific term such as "meat" or "meat meal," you can bet these are the lowest quality ingredients allowed. These ingredients are leftovers from slaughterhouses—the parts humans won't eat. They can also include leftover, expired meat from the grocery store or diseased livestock. Look for specific meat terms you recognize on your dog's food, such as turkey, beef, salmon, lamb or chicken.

If your dog food contains salmon or salmon meal, make sure it's labeled "wild-caught." Farm-raised salmon is less nutrient-dense than its wild counterpart because of the unnatural diet the fish are fed and has been found to potentially contain more contaminants.

NITRITES AND NITRATES – Chemical additives used to preserve freshness and extend the shelf life of meat products, nitrates and nitrites are found in human and dog food. Sodium nitrite can be toxic to your dog in high doses and has been linked to cancer.

SOY – Soy is cheap and readily available. Dog food manufacturers may use it as an inexpensive way to boost the protein percentage of the food, but it can be difficult for your dog to digest and can cause gastrointestinal upset.

Other ingredients to avoid include meat by-products, sodium hexametaphosphate, food dyes, carrageenan, taurine, cellulose, artificial flavors and corn syrup. Dog food manufacturers dedicated to producing a quality, superior dog food will not contain these red-flag ingredients. Though high-quality dog foods can be a bit more expensive, the cost will be well worth it and may even save you money in vet bills in the long term by nourishing your Whoodle properly.

Grain-free dog food has been a recent trend. Some claim that because wolves in the wild don't consume more than a trace amount of grains, domesticated dogs shouldn't either. The truth is that dogs are not genetically identical to wolves and they have adapted to effectively utilize grains.

Grain-free dog food contains other plants instead of the grains. These include peas, lentils, potatoes and legumes. These plant sources provide the starch to make the kibble and an added protein boost, allowing the manufacturer to cut back on more expensive animal proteins. This can lead to a depletion of the amino acid taurine. Taurine is found in animal proteins but not in plant proteins, and the FDA has linked this to a rise of cardiomyopathy in dogs who have been fed a grain-free diet. It is best to discuss with your vet what food is best for your dog before following any food trend.

Categories of Dog Food

Commercial dog food, no matter what kind you choose, comes in three basic categories: puppy, adult and senior. Knowing the difference between these is crucial when it comes to choosing the right one for your Whoodle.

Puppies, adult dogs and senior dogs all have unique dietary needs. Puppies need more calories to support their growing bodies, as well as higher levels of protein and fat. Puppy food is formulated especially for dogs up to the age of 15 months, depending on the dog, taking into account the higher nutrient needs of a growing pup.

Adult dog food is formulated to satisfy the needs of a fully developed adult dog, typically 15 months and older. This food is not sufficient for a growing pup as it will not meet his nutritional needs.

Dog food formulated for senior dogs is both lower in calories and higher in fiber. This nutritional balance is made for senior dogs who may be a little less active than they once were. The lower caloric count can help counteract any weight gain in old age.

If you are choosing between quality commercial dog foods for your dog, make sure you choose the right one for his stage of development. If you aren't sure when to make the switch from one to the other, consult your vet for advice. Take into account your dog's lifestyle, activity level, and weight.

Stories from a Whoodle Owner

Willow

Willows Special Diet

Willow gets two meals a day: kibble with topper and some canned food in the morning, and rice and boiled chicken in the evening. She loves dessert, whether it's a frozen marrow bone filled with peanut butter or a round bully stick. After some experimenting, I figured out she likes her kibble dry. She also appreciates it when I heat everything in the microwave for 15 seconds.

But, like many Whoodles, Willow has a delicate stomach and experiences bouts of the runs on a regular basis. It's hard to know what causes it. It could be something she grabbed on the street, animal poop she ate upstate, or a couple of licks from a puddle or stream on the trail. Every time she gets tested for parasites, it comes out negative. That's why she gets rice at dinner – it's a good binder. A frozen Kong filled with whole plain yogurt helps, and so does a daily probiotic chew. A nutritionist I know advised against canned pumpkin, which is popular among some owners, saying it can actually cause loose stool. When she has the runs, on walks I bring newspaper to put under her when she poops so she doesn't leave a mess that's hard to clean up.

Homemade Dog Food

Dogs should have a high-protein diet, limiting quantities of wheat, corn and soy. For optimal health, skip the kibble and make your dog a home-made, nutrition-packed meal at home. This is the only real way to know exactly what your dog is eating.

If you have the time and resources, homemade dog food can provide your Whoodle with a wonderful source of balanced nutrition, including real, whole foods without the preservatives commonly found in commercial foods. In addition, due to the high temperature used during processing

Photo Courtesy of Kris Jackson

causing significant loss of nutrients, food cooked at home is much more nutrient rich.

Many homemade dog food recipes using common kitchen ingredients, such as chicken, rice and vegetables, can be found online, but it's important that you discuss specific recipes with your vet to be sure they provide your dog with all of the nutrients he needs. Individual breeds and even dogs of the same breed can have different nutritional needs. When making your dog's food yourself, it's important to get a professional opinion regarding ingredients and serving size. Guessing and getting it wrong can be detrimental for your dog's health.

How Often Should I Feed My Whoodle?

When you bring your Whoodle home, it's important you continue his established feeding schedule using his current food so you do not cause stomach issues. Most veterinarians recommend feeding a young puppy, 5 to 6 months and under, 3 to 4 times a day. Slowly transition your Whoodle to once or twice-a-day feedings as they approach 6 months of age. Although some pet owners leave food out for dogs to graze on as they please, this is not recommended. If you have multiple pets in the house, it's impossible to know who is and who isn't eating properly.

If your dog is scarfing down his meal too quickly, this can cause regurgitation or vomiting. If your Whoodle is a fast eater, you may want to spread his food out into at least two meals a day. You can also invest in a slow feeder. These bowls are designed to slow your dog down with obstacles or columns that he has to eat around.

Table Food – What Is Good, What Is Not

When feeding your Whoodle food from your table, you must know what is safe and what is not. In Chapter 3, we discussed a list of foods to never feed your dog, so you may want to return there and refresh your memory before continuing on to this list of foods that are okay to share with your pup. While feeding your dog table food may seem cute and fun now, bad habits such as begging form quickly and are not easy to break.

If you choose to share food, there are a number of things you can safely share with your dog from your kitchen as a special treat or snack, but remember that these should be given in moderation so that they don't upset the balance of your dog's nutrition. None of these items should be heavily seasoned, as this may cause your dog an upset stomach.

- White and brown rice
- Cooked eggs
- Oatmeal
- Carrots
- Cheese (It is possible for some dogs to be lactose intolerant.)
- Peanut butter (without xylitol)
- Berries
- Green beans
- Seedless watermelon
- Bananas
- Peas
- Pineapple
- Apples
- Broccoli
- Potatoes

This is not a comprehensive list and food sensitivities can differ from dog to dog, so consult your veterinarian if you think your Whoodle may have a food allergy or sensitivity.

Weight Management

Weight management is as important for dogs as it is for humans. An overweight Whoodle can become susceptible to more disease and illness. If your dog is overweight, deal with the problem immediately.

One way you can help your dog maintain a healthy weight is by increasing his activity level in a safe way. Consult Chapter 8 for ideas to make exercise fun for you and your dog.

Also, consider what kind of nutrition your Whoodle is getting. Is he eating a quality commercial food? Low-quality foods are not healthy and contain filler ingredients that will fill your dog up temporarily without providing adequate nutrients. Your dog may end up eating more of these foods to make up for the lack of nutrition, causing weight issues.

If you prepare homemade dog food for your Whoodle and he is overweight, you need to go back to the vet or nutritionist to reevaluate ingredients and portion sizes. Also consider what your dog is eating when it isn't mealtime. Moderation is the key to sharing special treats. If weight is an issue for your dog, cut out the snacks and feed him only at designated mealtimes.

If you can't get your dog's weight under control by limiting snacks, providing him with quality food, and exercise, discuss options with your vet. He or she may suggest a weight-management food featuring higher than average protein, lower than average fat and fewer calories. These foods are formulated for adult dogs only and should never be given to a puppy. Remember to read food labels and choose a food made with high-quality ingredients.

How to Handle a Picky Eater

While most dogs seem to gobble up anything you put in front of them, including things they weren't supposed to eat, some dogs are just downright picky. If you find yourself with a Whoodle who isn't too keen on eating what you put in front of him, here are a few things you can do to encourage him to eat.

1. REMOVE HIS FOOD. If your dog is turning up his nose to his food, try taking it away. Feed him as usual but give him only 15 minutes to eat his meal. If he hasn't started eating within 15 minutes or he has walked away, pick up his food and wait until his next scheduled mealtime to feed him again. Repeat this for every meal until he eats. Your Whoodle should soon get the idea that he needs to eat while his food is available.

2. ADD A TOPPER. There are many toppers on the market designed to mix in with your dog's food to make it more enticing. Make sure these toppers are thoroughly mixed in, coating every bit of food so that your Whoodle doesn't simply eat the topper and not the food.

3. SWITCH IT UP. As mentioned several times, you should never abruptly change your Whoodle's food. However, if you find your dog isn't interested in the food in his bowl, you may want to slowly transition him to a new kind or flavor. If he's turning his nose up to chicken, try a fish-flavored food. If he's not into salmon, try lamb. Remember to transition by mixing foods over time before weaning him off the original completely.

If your dog has suddenly become a reluctant eater, schedule an appointment with the vet to rule out illness or injury. Sometimes lack of appetite can be the first sign something isn't quite right.

CHAPTER 14

Dealing with Unwanted Behaviors

What Is Considered Bad Behavior?

Dog personalities vary as much as human personalities—no two are alike. While a well-trained, obedient dog is the goal, even successful training won't keep a spunky dog from being spunky. Just like humans, dogs can exhibit annoying behaviors that are not necessarily bad. So, when it comes to bad habits and behaviors, what is and is not actually considered "bad" and in need of correcting?

BARKING – Barking is as natural for your dog as speaking is to you and should never be considered bad behavior. Whoodles are not known for being chatty and don't bark as frequently as other breeds, however, it may be something that becomes an issue in certain circumstances. If so, there are measures you can take to correct the annoyance.

First, find the cause of the barking. Is there a direct, consistent trigger, such as seeing other people or dogs? If this is the case, socialization is key for teaching your dog to remain calm among other dogs or people. If the problem is more inconsistent, consider whether your Whoodle may simply be trying to get your attention in those moments. Are you spending enough time with your dog meeting his physical and emotional needs?

Though uncommon for this breed, if your Whoodle has a problem with excessive barking, fill a soda bottle halfway with rocks or coins and shake it every time he barks. Tell him "quiet" in a calm voice and reward him with a small treat when he stops. Continue this method until he learns to be "quiet" on command.

If barking while you are away is an issue, see the section on Separation Anxiety in Chapter 5 for ways to keep your Whoodle calm while you are gone. While some owners resort to vocal cord operations such as devocalization, or shock collars to keep their dogs quiet, these are cruel punishments for a canine behavior that isn't inherently bad.

CHASING – Whoodles are instinctually wired to chase things. While this behavior can become an issue, and be particularly annoying, it should never be treated as "bad" behavior. Your dog is only doing what comes naturally to him. Obedience training can help this issue but it may never become eliminated completely.

While not bad, chasing can indeed become dangerous if not kept in check. Whether your Whoodle is chasing a skateboarder through the city or a deer through a rural area, his chasing instinct can get him into significant trouble. Unless you are certain he can control his urge to chase and remain by your side on command, it may never be safe for your Whoodle to be off-leash in an unfenced area. Not only are the objects of his chase a potential danger, so are cars and other hazards.

Photo Courtesy of Cabrina Little

Stories from a Whoodle Owner

Flynn

Taming the Chase

When Flynn was less than 18 months old, he scared us to death by taking off from a get-together in a friend's back yard chasing a Harley-Davidson that had slowed down for the curve. We took off after him, calling frantically, and a few minutes later he did indeed reappear, tongue hanging out and clearly very proud of himself. After that he became obsessed with motorcycles; he could hear them from miles away, and watched them avidly anytime we came across one. We ramped up attendance at the local training classes, but it quickly became clear to us that Flynn thought treat-based recall lessons were fun, but catching a motorcycle was his calling. We were frantic; we wanted a dog that could be reliably off-leash on our country rambles, so we went searching for a more effective solution. We interviewed trainers from many different schools, and tried various classes and techniques. Finally, we found our solution with a trainer whose focus was field dogs (dogs trained for bird-hunting), but who had given in to the desperate pleas for help from people like us. Fortunately for us, he was willing to train pets whose owners wouldn't know what to do with a grouse (or, say, a wild turkey) if it landed in their laps. I interviewed him (really, I grilled him) without Flynn, and when I was finally convinced and brought Flynn for his first lesson, he looked at him and said, "Yep, that's a dog". Flynn immediately adored him, and that opinion deepened in the weeks of tough work that our trainer put him through.

Flynn is a typical Whoodle--smart, self-confident, and occasionally a bit stubborn. He learns quickly, but if things don't stay interesting, he'll innovate to keep the lesson challenging...for everyone. We had gone to Puppy Class, and Recall Class, and Polite Greetings, and Agility, and several other classes with fun and exciting names. Flynn quickly learned what was expected, and either excelled at the lesson, or raised the ante to make it more exciting. After all, why get up onto a high plank walk just to walk sedately to the other end, when you can launch off the middle and get back to the more exciting agility jumps? Now, Flynn had finally met a trainer who wouldn't let him get away with these antics, and he blossomed with the discipline.

We started with drop-in lessons teaching me to teach Flynn, but after a couple of months of slow progress we decided to board Flynn with the professional trainer for focused work. Two weeks later, "sit" had transformed from his butt more or less grazing the ground to slapping down like a rubber band was attached. And most importantly of all, we had a dog with rock-solid recall. Flynn thrived at the kennel, loved every minute of his training, and now joyfully runs over and stretches out his neck for his collar when he hears the beep of it being turned on. Yes, an electric collar was the answer, and what a great solution it has been.

Flynn is still smart, self-confident, and occasionally a bit stubborn. He is also a very happy pup. He gets loads of exercise with his collar out in the woods or without his collar at the dog park where he is everyone's favorite playmate for a rousing game of chase or tug-of-war. And those motorcycles? He no longer cares; a bicycle, Kawasaki, or Harley gets no more than a glance, because there's much more fun to be had going where we're going. He is still disappointed that I have no interest in turkeys, but within the generous limits I set and enforce, he gets to follow his nose wherever it might take him. The collar is always there for support if we need it, but we only need to use it to get his attention on the rare occasions when he's seriously distracted by a bolting rabbit, or fox, or turkey, or deer. His collar allows us to interrupt that prey-chase reaction, and reminds him that his most important job is to be our beloved pet, walking with us on the trail.

DIGGING – Whoodles love to dig! Much like chasing, digging is a natural behavior and may involve rolling around in the freshly disturbed dirt. This is not bad behavior, but it can become annoying and may be curbed with stricter supervision and obedience training. See Chapter 5 for more information on how to deal with a digging Whoodle.

LEASH PULLING – This is a direct result of improper or inadequate training and is not bad behavior. Your Whoodle simply does not know what you expect of him while on a leash. Teach your dog the proper way to walk on a leash and this problem can be eliminated. Do not let this issue go uncorrected as it can lead to injury for your Whoodle or for you.

If you're dealing with a leash-pulling Whoodle, the first thing you need is a harness to help ease the strain and give you more control. This will allow you to more effectively and comfortably guide your dog on your walks. If your Whoodle is pulling the leash because he is over excited, try a game of fetch in your living room or backyard before hooking him up to the leash. This can help him get some energy out and may help him be calmer on the leash.

When leash training, take your Whoodle to a familiar area with little to no distractions. Have treats handy and practice getting your dog to look at you while standing still on the leash. Refer to Chapter 9 for more information on the "look" command. As your dog remains calm and attentive to you, walk him slowly, still commanding him to look at you, back and forth down a small stretch. Reward your dog for calm and attentive walking, redirecting his attention back to you if he becomes excited or distracted. With practice, your Whoodle will be a master at walking calmly on a leash.

Photo Courtesy of
Rebecca Watson

Other unwanted behaviors that are not considered "bad" include destroying toys, chewing up shoes, begging or stealing food, jumping on people, getting on furniture and eating poop. All of these behaviors can be a nuisance but are typically not evidence of a poorly behaved dog. If you are dealing with these issues, address them with proper training as discussed in Chapter 9.

HELPFUL TIP
Satisfying the Prey Drive

Wheaten Terriers and Poodles both typically have a high prey drive, meaning that your Whoodle might also. Prey drive is a dog's instinct to hunt and capture prey, which could be a neighborhood squirrel or the family cat. It's important to teach your dog self-control when it comes to this drive, but some dog owners find that indulging their dog's prey drive in a controlled environment can go a long way toward curbing it. Activities such as fetch, Frisbee, prey-stick play, or even blowing bubbles to chase are a great way to play into your dog's desire to hunt. Make sure to establish cues for your dog to show when it's time to start and stop this kind of play.

AGGRESSION – Behavior that should always be considered "bad" is any form of unprovoked aggression. This could be vicious growling, biting, lunging or snarling directly at other animals, people and even children. These behaviors are unacceptable and can result in serious injury or death for your dog or the object of his aggression. This includes food or possession aggression.

Swift and immediate action must be taken to correct this type of behavior. There may be a root issue or trigger that you are not aware of, so consult a professional trainer or animal psychologist promptly if you are dealing with these dangerous dog behaviors.

HUMAN AGGRESSION – A Whoodle that is aggressive toward people is typically due to a lack of socialization as a young puppy. It is so important to socialize your Whoodle from a very young age to remain calm around people of all ages. Without proper socialization, your Whoodle can become fearful of the noise or the quick and sporadic movements of a child.

If your Whoodle is older and has developed aggression through a bad experience or a lack of socialization, reach out to a trainer or behaviorist to address the problem immediately. This is potentially a matter of life or death for your dog so do not delay professional help.

Photo Courtesy of
Bill Burton

RESOURCE AGGRESSION: While resource aggression, also sometimes called food aggression, is a major problem for some dogs, it is actually an instinctually driven reaction. This behavior has been passed through generations of evolution and it stems from your dog simply needing to protect his limited resources. Your Whoodle may be protective over his food, his toys or his treats. Though instinctive, this behavior is extremely dangerous and can escalate quickly, leading to injury for anyone who comes near, especially children who may not know any better.

> **FUN FACT**
> **Best in Show**
>
> 
>
> Whoodles aren't able to compete in the Westminster Kennel Club Dog Show, but their parent breeds are! As of 2020, a standard Poodle has won Best in Show at the annual Westminster Kennel Club Dog Show a total of five times. The first Poodle winner, in 1935, was named Ch. Nunsoe Duc de la Terrace of Blakeen. Most recently a Poodle named GCHP Stone Run Afternoon Tea took home the title in 2020. A Miniature Poodle has won the title three times, and a Toy Poodle has won twice. As of 2020, a soft-coated Wheaten Terrier hasn't yet won Best in Show.

Luckily, food and resource aggression is not a common trait in Whoodles, but there is still a chance your dog may deal with this issue at some point. Aside from a genetic predisposition in some of the more dominant dog breeds, trauma, such as loss of an owner, abuse and even natural disasters can also trigger food aggression.

Before tackling food aggression on your own, determine the severity of the aggression. A mild aggression may present itself through verbal warnings, such as growling and baring teeth when you approach. Moderate aggression may present as a dog physically lunging or snapping at a human or another animal that gets too close. Severe resource aggression may involve significant physical contact, such as biting and chasing until the threat goes away. If you are dealing with moderate to severe resource aggression, you may want to reach out to a professional for help before things get out of hand.

If your Whoodle is displaying mild forms of resource aggression with toys or bones, begin with the steps below to eradicate the issue.

1. To successfully redirect a possessive dog, he must first learn the command "leave it." See Chapter 9 for more information and a step-by-step method for mastery.
2. Begin the training by giving your dog a toy or bone that he is typically possessive over. Using training treats, give him the "leave it" command and offer him a treat away from the toy. If he is reluctant to leave his

possession for a training treat, offer him small bits of real meat, such as deli turkey. As your dog comes away from his possession for the treat, carefully reach down and pick up the toy while he is occupied.

3. Praise him verbally and with a treat after you have successfully removed the possession.
4. Carefully extend the toy or bone out to your dog and let him lick or take it from your hand. You are communicating to him that you are not a threat and you are not trying to take it from him. Once he has the toy back, continue the same process to remove it again. Do this until your dog is calmly and willingly relinquishing his toy in exchange for a treat.

If your Whoodle is displaying mild forms of food aggression, take these steps to desensitize him and get him more comfortable with your presence while he is eating.

1. Stand in the room with your Whoodle while he is eating. Get as close as your dog will let you without showing aggression. While he is eating, speak calmly and cheerfully to him to show him you are not a threat. Try and pick a key phrase for him to become familiar with such as, "How's the food, bud? Is it good?"
2. As your Whoodle becomes accustomed to you in the area, give him a tasty treat while he is eating. Approach him calmly and offer a high-value treat, such as deli meat, in the area where he is eating. Do this repeatedly for several days to reinforce the idea that good things happen when you approach his feeding space.
3. Once your dog is comfortable with step two, progress to tossing his high-value treat into his bowl as he is eating. Be sure you get your dog's attention and show him the treat before you toss it into the bowl. Repeat this until he comfortably allows you to add the treat to his bowl of food, again, reinforcing the idea that good things happen when you go near his food.

Keep practicing these steps until your Whoodle is calm as you approach his eating area and even his bowl of food. Depending on your dog, this process may be quick or it may take a bit of time. If your dog relapses at any point and becomes aggressive, you may have progressed too quickly and need to take a step back. Remember, food aggression can get more severe if action is not taken to correct the issue so seek professional help if your Whoodle is not making progress.

Finding the Root of the Problem

The first step to eliminating the issue of any unwanted behavior, benign or not, is finding the cause. Learning why makes correcting the problem easier for both you and your dog.

INSTINCTUAL – If the unwanted behavior you are dealing with is something instinctually bred into your dog, it will probably be more difficult to correct. Try training with a professional, but if that doesn't work, you may have to redirect the unwanted behavior into an appropriate outlet.

For example, if your dog loves to chase, as most Whoodles do, find him a way to chase safely in a controlled environment. This applies to all instinctual issues, including chewing and digging. Allow your dog to do these things in a way that is safe and appropriate.

LACK OF TRAINING – The majority of a dog's unwanted behaviors stem from a simple lack of training. Leash tugging, jumping, begging for food and jumping on furniture are all a direct result of inconsistent boundaries set by the owner. Training your dog consistently and purposefully is the best way to correct these unwanted behaviors. See Chapter 9 for tips on where to get started.

If you are dealing with a real aggression issue with your Whoodle, determine the root cause. Aggression is not a trait of a healthy and happy Whoodle so there is probably an underlying issue at play. Could he be suffering from a health issue? Is there a traumatic event in your dog's past? A long-standing lack of socialization? If so, there may be a long road ahead. You will more than likely require the assistance of a trainer and possibly a dog psychologist. These behavioral issues can be a matter of life or death for a dog, so approach them with intention and purpose.

How to Properly Correct Your Dog

Research has made clear that punishment is not an effective way to correct a dog. Unless your dog has had a trauma in his past or a medical condition, he will generally want to please you with his actions. Correct him by showing him what you want him to do instead of punishing the unwanted behavior. Revisit Chapter 9 for more information on positive reinforcement methods and the dangers of correcting by punishment.

If you are dealing with an issue that does not concern safety, but rather annoyance, do your best to meet your dog in the middle with a solution that will make you both happy. If he loves to chew, keep a steady supply of interesting chew toys at his disposal so that he can still chew, but you don't have to worry about your belongings. If he loves digging, allow him to do so safely without destroying your garden.

Stories from a Whoodle Owner

Willow

Willow's High Prey Drive

Willow is the perfect dog – friendly, happy, curious, affectionate, funny – except for one thing. She's a chaser – it's in her DNA. Because we spend time both in the city and the country, she's seen, and chased, it all. In the city she goes after bicycles, motorbikes, scooters, skateboards, roller-skaters and runners. In the country, its runners and bikers on the hiking trail, as well as every type of animal imaginable. She also chases cars when she's in the mood.

This means Willow cannot be off leash: she would follow her "prey" right into the next state. We hired a behaviorist and are making some progress, mostly by distracting her with high-value treats. The ultimate goal is to have her turn to us for a treat as soon as she sees something that she wants to chase. We also work on recall. She's only two, so there's still a long road ahead. We're keeping our fingers crossed that eventually we will be able to help her control her instincts.

When to Call a Professional

Behaviors that may appear harmless can become a dangerous issue for your dog if not addressed. Digging can be harmless if it leads only to a few holes in the backyard, but if it evolves into digging under the fence, it can become a serious problem. Likewise, losing a few pairs of shoes is frustrating but not dangerous. However, if a chewer decides to eat a loose electrical cord or a toy with small batteries, it could end in an emergency trip to the animal hospital.

If you are unable to redirect your dog's behavior yourself, in a safe and controlled way, contact your local dog training facility and ask for help. They will have the resources and tools to help you find a solution that works for you and your dog. It's important to seek help at the first sign of a problem to prevent dangerous escalation. If you do wait until habits form, it will be much harder to correct the behavior.

If basic obedience training is not stopping the problematic behavior, consider contacting a dog behaviorist. While behaviorists know how to train dogs, they also have vast knowledge of each breed's behavior allowing him or her to analyze the possible psychological reasons for the behavior. The first thing a dog behaviorist will need from you is extensive background information on your Whoodle and a full scope of his diet, lifestyle and any other factors you may deem important. A behaviorist will work together with both you and your Whoodle to find out why the behavior is happening, if there are any underlying issues, and how to correct it in an effective way.

Photo Courtesy of Valerie Sheridan

CHAPTER 15

Caring for Your Senior Whoodle

A smaller sized Whoodle is considered "senior" around the age of 10 or 11. As a general rule, smaller dogs typically have a longer life expectancy so if your Whoodle is medium sized or larger, he will reach his senior years sooner, around the age of 8 or 9.

Caring for an aging dog can present a whole new set of challenges. Aging dogs, just like humans, typically require more medical care because they are prone to ailments such as arthritis, cognitive dysfunction, cataracts, hearing loss, incontinence and the inability to regulate body temperature.

Not all dogs reach this stage at the same time, and many live comfortable and happy lives for years, even with these ailments. This chapter will discuss potential issues you may face with your aging dog and help you navigate the difficult end-of-life decisions when the time comes.

Photo Courtesy of Sarah Ryan

Common Old-Age Ailments

ARTHRITIS – Osteoarthritis is a degenerative joint disease where the bones of a joint rub against each other due to the deterioration of the cartilage between them. This deterioration can cause severe pain, stiffness and limited mobility. Osteoarthritis cannot be cured, but it can be treated with medication and supplements to treat symptoms and slow the progression of the disease.

If your Whoodle develops arthritis, keeping him comfortable is important. Items such as an orthopedic bed, a ramp to access furniture or a bed and even rugs on slippery floors can all go a long way in easing his discomfort.

HELPFUL TIP
Identifying Retinal Atrophy

Whoodles are considered an overall healthy breed, but there are several diseases to keep an eye out for. One of these is called progressive retinal atrophy, a hereditary condition that can affect Poodles as well as many other breeds. Signs that your dog may be suffering from this disease include:

- Difficulty seeing in low or bright light
- Inability to locate toys
- Bumping into objects
- Blindness
- Getting lost at night

If you suspect that your dog is experiencing a vision issue, visit your vet for further testing. There is no cure for this disease, but it isn't painful, and there are many resources for helping your dog cope with blindness.

CATARACTS – Cataracts create an opacity in a dog's normally clear lens, causing his vision to blur. If your senior dog develops cataracts, have your vet monitor him closely for worsening symptoms. Cloudiness in your dog's lenses is the most obvious sign of cataracts, however, you may notice signs of vision loss as well. These may include clumsiness and difficulty navigating familiar areas.

The only treatment for cataracts is surgery. This operation is very similar to the one performed on humans to remove cataracts. If you can afford it or are willing to spend the money on the costly surgery, this operation can greatly improve your dog's quality of life in his final years. If left untreated, cataracts can lead to blindness. While this is not a death sentence for your Whoodle, it would be a major life adjustment for you and him. That said, many blind dogs live happy and healthy lives!

COGNITIVE DYSFUNCTION – Cognitive dysfunction, also known as dementia, is common in senior dogs just like it is in senior humans. If you notice your dog forgetting something he does often or acting unusually out of his normal routine, notify your vet and discuss options to improve his quality of life. Making everyday tasks simpler for him can help ease frustration. This may mean putting his food and water in a more visible place in the house, leading him outside more often or using a puppy pad to avoid accidents, and keeping his toys and belongings easily accessible.

Just like with humans, dogs with cognitive dysfunction can benefit greatly from mental stimulation. Continue to review and practice basic commands such as sit and stay with your senior dog or play a basic game of hide and seek with a toy. These activities can help to slow the progression of this condition and can help improve memory.

HEARING LOSS – Hearing loss is common in senior dogs. While many will lose some degree of hearing, not all dogs go deaf in old age. Signs of hearing loss include a sudden lack of obedience, increased startle reaction and excessive barking. If you notice these symptoms in your Whoodle, first see a vet to rule out other causes such as waxy buildup in the ears.

If your dog experiences hearing loss due to old age, you may need to find another way to communicate with him. Teach your dog hand signals

Photo Courtesy of Kelli and Kevin Hesseltine

at the first sign of hearing loss so that if he loses his hearing completely, you can still communicate commands. It may also be helpful to keep a flashlight handy to signal for his attention. Some deaf dogs can become anxious if they don't know where you are, so make it a habit to get your dog's attention before you leave a room.

If your dog becomes deaf, you may want to attach a safety device to him in the event he becomes lost. This could be something simple like a bell you can hear or even a GPS tag. This could save your dog's life if he is ever separated from you.

FUN FACT
Oldest Toy Poodle

Whoodles have an average life span of 12 to 15 years. While a Whoodle has yet to make headlines for its longevity, a Poodle nearly made it into the Guinness World Records by living approximately 25 years. Uncle Chichi, a Toy Poodle from New York City, was adopted from an animal shelter when he was one or two years old and lived a further 24 years with his owners, Frank Pavich and Janet Puhalovic. Toy Poodles have a slightly longer life expectancy than their larger counterparts, which might mean that Whoodles who are bred from a Toy Poodle may also have slightly longer lives

Basic Senior Dog Care

Care for a senior Whoodle should focus on keeping him comfortable and happy. Much like people, senior dogs have trouble regulating their body temperatures. Be sure to provide your dog with extra warmth on a cold day and make sure he stays cool on a hot day.

Special accommodations may need to be made to make life more comfortable for your senior dog. If he has arthritis, he may benefit from a specially made bed to help with stiffness. If you have stairs, you may also need to consider keeping all of your dog's things on the lowest level of your home. This will keep him from needing to climb the stairs, potentially causing him unneeded strain and discomfort.

As a dog ages, energy levels usually decline along with stamina. Even so, it's important that you still give your aging Whoodle regular, gentle exercise to keep him in shape. Avoid intense physical activity and don't push your senior Whoodle too hard or you risk serious injury or other health issues such as overheating.

Obesity can be a problem in older dogs, who typically move around less, and it can exacerbate other age-related ailments such as arthritis and heart conditions. If obesity becomes a problem despite regular exercise, discuss options with your veterinarian. He or she may suggest switching to a different food.

Often, a dog's dental care is neglected throughout life, leading to potentially painful issues in old age. If your elderly dog suddenly seems to lose his appetite, check with your vet to see if the problem could be dental. Sometimes a painful tooth or painful gums can be enough to deter a dog from his dinner.

Your senior dog will probably need to see the vet more during his last years than he did previously. The American Animal Hospital Association (AAHA) recommends that you take your senior dog to the vet at least once

Photo Courtesy of Tracey McCloskey

every six months for a check-up. These regular vet visits can help you catch any conditions early and allow for more prompt treatment, potentially leading to a better quality of life for your dog.

Illness and Injury Prevention

One of the most important aspects of senior dog care is preventing illness and injury. It's much more challenging for an elderly dog to overcome an illness or injury than it is for a younger dog.

As discussed above, exercise is just as important for a senior dog. It should look a little different, though. Because a senior dog is more prone to injury, exercise should be done at a less vigorous pace that will have less impact on aging joints. A slow walk or a swim are great options for senior dogs. Avoid anything that involves jumping or climbing as these activities risk injury or aggravation of arthritis.

Mental exercise is just as, if not more, important for a senior dog. Continue obedience training or practice into the senior years to keep his mind sharp and active. This may help prevent or slow cognitive decline.

To protect your senior dog from illness, be sure to continue his parasite medication for fleas and ticks. Also, make sure he stays up to date on his vaccinations. If an elderly dog does fall ill, he is more likely to suffer complications that may be life-threatening. A younger dog may contract the common Bordetella bacterium and suffer no real consequences, but for a senior dog, a simple infection can quickly turn into pneumonia, which may result in a hospital stay or even death.

Supplements and Nutrition

Proper nutrition, including supplementation, is more important than ever when a dog reaches his golden years. Quality of life and severity of geriatric conditions can be greatly influenced by nutrition. There are many supplements on the market that are specifically formulated for senior dogs.

Before adding any supplement to your dog's diet, consult your veterinarian. He or she may be able to direct you to a quality brand or alert you to possible side effects or interactions with your dog's current medications.

Below is a list of the most common supplements.

GLUCOSAMINE AND CHONDROITIN – Two supplements often paired together to combat osteoarthritis, glucosamine and chondroitin have been found to be therapeutic in the treatment of canine arthritis. These compounds are found naturally in cartilage and are made by the body.

When seeking a glucosamine and chondroitin supplement, look for highly reputable brands that source all of their ingredients from the United States. Imported glucosamine has been found to contain many contaminants, including lead, especially when sourced from China. Since the FDA does not regulate supplements, the only way to know if you are getting a quality product is to be vigilant and diligent in your research. Even popular pet store brands that say "made in the USA" can include ingredients sourced from China.

OMEGA-3 FATTY ACIDS – Omega-3 fatty acids like DHA and EPA have been shown to be beneficial in many ways that may support the health of your senior dog. These fatty acids are good for the brain, potentially improving cognitive function in old age and may even give your Whoodle's immune system a boost. According to the American Kennel Club, "The addition of omega-3 to the diet may [also] help reduce inflammation and can promote cell membrane health."

ANTIOXIDANTS – Including an extra source of antioxidants in your senior dog's diet can be beneficial as well. You can do this by purchasing a supplement or by simply allowing your dog to snack on high antioxidant fruits, such as berries and apples.

PROBIOTICS – Probiotics help maintain healthy bacteria in the gut, the place where up to 80 percent of a dog's immune defenses reside. This can improve immune function and help your senior dog ward off illness and disease more efficiently.

CBD – Also known as cannabidiol, CBD is a supplement that offers many potential benefits for an aging dog. It has been shown to ease pain, ease anxiety and even fight cancer. This can be of great benefit to a Whoodle that is dealing with painful arthritis or one that has become anxious due to loss of sight, hearing or anything else. Be sure to purchase a CBD oil that is made specifically for dogs and follow dosing instructions carefully. Always talk to your vet before changing your Whoodle's diet and supplements.

When It's Time to Say Goodbye

The hardest part of being a pet owner is knowing when it's time to say goodbye. Our dogs devote the best years of their lives to us, unconditionally gifting us with love and loyalty, no matter the circumstances. When you see that your beloved Whoodle is experiencing more pain than joy, it may be time to consider the most difficult decision pet owners face.

Many believe it is one of the worst and greatest responsibilities of animal ownership to know when to humanely relieve an animal from the pain when the end of the animal's life is inevitable. It is never an easy decision and often leads to an array of emotions for the owner, including sorrow, guilt and second thoughts. Preparing yourself early on to navigate the emotions that come along with saying goodbye may help eliminate confusion when the time comes.

How Will You Know When the Time Is Right?

No one knows your dog better than you do and no one will be able to make this decision for you. You and your Whoodle have a bond that nobody else can understand and that is exactly what makes you the right person to make the final call. If you have a gut feeling that your senior dog has had a sharp decline in health and is hurting more than he is enjoying life, talk to your vet. As hard as it may be, it may be time to say goodbye.

A few telltale signs that death is imminent in a senior dog are extreme lethargy, lack of interest in anything, loss of coordination, incontinence and not eating or drinking.

Only you and your dog will know when this time is. Your dog has trusted you with his life during all the time you spent together and he trusts you with it now. If you believe putting him down humanely will end his suffering, speak to your vet and discuss euthanasia.

Once you have made the decision that the time has come to humanely end your dog's suffering, understand that second thoughts are normal. Grieving over this decision is natural and normal. Talk to a trusted friend or family member to help you cope during this difficult time.

Once you have made the decision, as long as the vet agrees that death is inevitable, the process happens fairly quickly. The point is to end your dog's suffering, so there is no reason to delay.

Natural Death

Euthanasia is not the only option if your dog is showing signs of death. While many owners believe it is the only way to end a dog's suffering, you can allow your Whoodle to die a natural death in the comfort of his own home. Pain management and comfort are key for allowing your dog to die a natural death. If pain cannot be controlled and comfort is impossible, reconsider your decision for a natural death and talk to your vet about euthanasia. It is not fair to prolong your Whoodle's suffering simply to add a few days to his life.

The Euthanasia Process

Some vets offer to come to your home to perform the euthanasia there, while others will want you to bring your dog into the clinic. Either way, you will have the option to be present when the vet performs the procedure.

Before you take your dog to the vet, call any friends or family members who may want to say goodbye. Although it may be hard for you to watch your dog die, know that it will bring your dog comfort and peace in his last moments. Hold him and comfort him just as you have for your entire lives together.

Photo Courtesy Of Sharon Corodimas

During the procedure, your vet will administer a solution, typically phenobarbital, intravenously. The solution is usually thick with a blue, pink, or purple tint. The vet may inject it directly into a vein or into an intravenous catheter. Once the solution is injected, it will quickly travel through your dog's body, causing him to lose consciousness within just a few seconds. Your Whoodle will feel no pain. Breathing will slow then stop altogether. Cardiac arrest will occur and cause death within 30 seconds of the injection.

Your vet will check for signs of life and will most likely step out of the room so you can say a final goodbye. Your vet and the office staff have been through this before and understand the emotional weight of the situation. They should provide you with privacy and be a source of comfort if needed. Be sure to make payments and after-death arrangements beforehand so that you don't have to deal with it in the aftermath.

Your dog's body may still move after death, so don't be alarmed if you see twitching. He may also release bodily fluids, which is also normal.

Final Arrangements

Cremation is a common option for those who want to memorialize their beloved Whoodle. It is more economical than finding a plot in a pet cemetery and it's a relatively simple process. If you have chosen to have your dog cremated, your vet will coordinate with a funeral home or cremation service and notify you when his ashes are ready.

If you are taking your deceased dog home for burial, the vet will place your dog's remains in a container and will typically carry it out to the car for you. Though burying your pet at home is legal in most states, it may not be the best idea. When burying a pet at home, be aware that your dog's remains could resurface due to a flood, be dug up by a wild animal, or even contaminate the soil and groundwater with dangerous bacteria. If you choose to have a memorial at your home, consider spreading his ashes there instead of a burial.

A pet cemetery is another option for a final resting place for your Whoodle. This is a designated graveyard for pets to be buried safely. This service is pricey and costs around $400 to $600 just for the plot. Casket prices vary in addition to those fees. While it is an expensive option, your Whoodle will rest in a beautiful area among other loved pets.

Whichever you choose, once you leave the vet's office you will begin the grieving process. Hold on to the love and memories you share and your loving Whoodle will never be forgotten.

CPSIA information can be obtained
at www.ICGtesting.com
Printed in the USA
LVHW070309200821
695739LV00001B/3

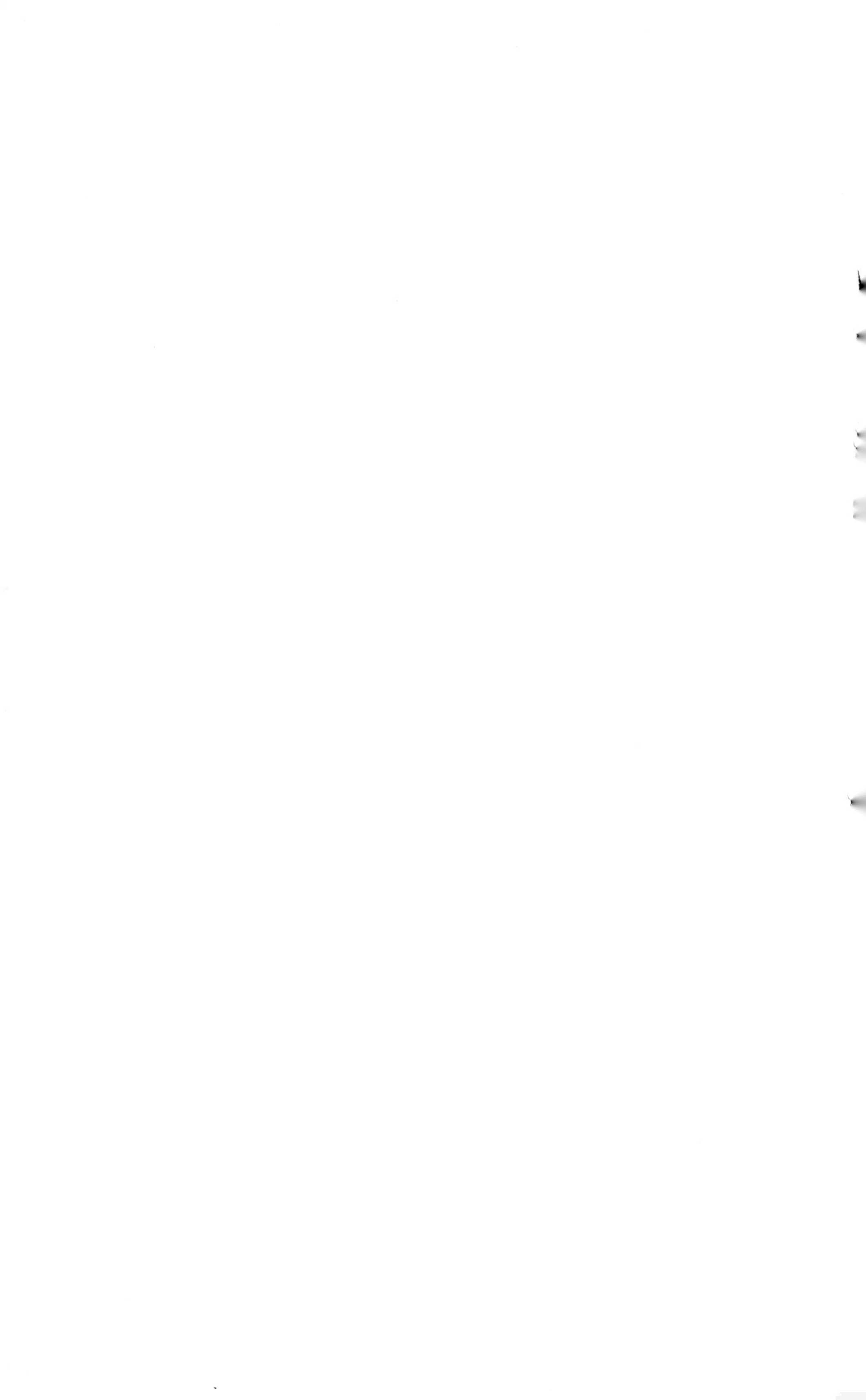